# THE BLUE GROVE

# THE
# BLUE GROVE
## THE POETRY OF THE
# URAONS

*by*
**W.G. Archer**
*with a Foreword*
*by*
**Arthur Waley**

**GYAN PUBLISHING HOUSE**
**NEW DELHI-110002**

The Blue Grove

Rs. 450

ISBN: 81-212-0888-2



Published in 2006 in India by
Gyan Publishing House
5, Ansari Road, Darya Ganj, New Delhi-110002
Phones : 23282060, 23261060, Fax : 011-23285914
E-mail : gyanbook@vsnl.com
Website : http://www.gyanbooks.com

*Laser Typesetting at* : Shiva Infosystem, Delhi
*Printed at* : Salasar Imaging System, Delhi

To

ERNEST

BARKER

# FOREWORD

The author's main object in translating these songs was to convey as much as possible of their beauty. Thus the book ranks with Shamrao Hivale and Verrier Elwin's *Songs of the Forest*, in that it is one of the rare examples of Indian popular poetry put into English with sensitivity and skill. But Mr. Archer's *The Blue Grove* goes much further than any other work of the kind, in that he systematically relates the songs to the social activities with which they are connected; so that his book has a great ethnological value in addition to its importance simply as literature.

Very little attention has been paid by ethnologists to unwritten poetry. It has generally been considered a branch of "folk-lore", and as "folk-lore" has hitherto meant (with rare exceptions) the folk-lore of the West, we know very little about the songs of non-European peoples. The traditional poetry of the American Indians, studied in numerous publications of the American Bureau of Ethnology, forms perhaps the principal exception.

Ethnological interest goes in waves. Now it is skulls, now it is kinship terms, now it is "character-types". So far songs have never been the fashion. It is easy to substantiate this assertion. For example, the most recent general work on primitive life, Boas's *General Anthropology*, has only four or five pages on song, as opposed to a hundred pages on economic organization. The barest facts as to what kind of poetical technique exists in different areas of the world are not given, or are given wrong. It is said, for example,[1] that the epic is confined to "Europe and a considerable part of Central Asia". As the present tense is used, the omission of the Near East (the great Babylonian epics) may be justified. But the Indian epics are very much alive not only in India but also in Indonesia. And what about the Ainu epic, *The Golden Otter*, which is in every way an entirely typical specimen?

[1] P. 599.

Another proof of the lack of work upon traditional song is the fact that when in 1934 the Anthropological Congress was held in London, out of nearly a hundred papers there was not one which dealt specifically with song. It may of course be said that song is not a detachable, independent subject, and is bound up with music, dance, and other activities. But there were scores of papers which dealt with much narrower subjects; there was one, for example, on Aspects of Dentition.

Or take another test. I possess about a hundred and fifty books on ethnology. Only four or five of them mention singing, and there is not one which treats of it at all adequately.

I think I have proved that there is in ethnological literature ample room for such a work as Mr. Archer's.

This book also throws some light on an important problem, that of the intelligibility of primitive songs. For example, No. 104 speaks of the mainah-birds fighting and the mango being in bloom, but it makes no mention of the two groups of marriage-agents, who are the real subject of the song. We see in fact here and in other spheres of primitive song that in some cases the comparison is put side by side with the statement of the song, as in the Chinese :

The pelican stays on the bridge;
It has not wetted its beak.
That fine gentleman
Has not followed up his love-meeting.

Or the statement can be omitted altogether and only the comparison left. Another example from Mr. Archer's book of this omission of the real subject of the song is

In the corn fields, in the wheat fields
Parrots from other sides have gathered
The parrot of the house has flown
The parrot of the house has flown to the jungle
Parrots from other sides have gathered.

The subject of the poem is not parrots at all, but the departure of the bride.

One sees from such examples that unless the circumstances in which songs are used have been thoroughly explored and the stock imagery understood, many songs are likely to be classed as pointless or irrational, which are in reality full of the most precise and logical meaning. It is well known that as transmitted to us by ethnologists a great many primitive songs appear to be nonsensical. Indeed, Heinz Werner, in his *Ursprünge der Lyrik*, has put forward a theory of successive stages through which poetry passes. The songs of very primitive people are, according to him, merely unintelligible noises, those of people not quite so savage begin to harbour a little, vague meaning ; till we finally come to the entirely rational and explicit poetry of civilized communities.

I do not know whether any part of this theory is true. It is certain, at any rate, that the supposed irrationality of some primitive poetry is an illusion due to the fact that the transmitters have failed to relate the songs to the social system which produced them, failed to grasp the system of imagery employed, and failed in many cases to obtain a proper explanation of dialect words, archaisms, and euphonic distortions.

The lack of curiosity about poetical technique which ethnologists display is sometimes amazing. For example, a field-worker from Easter Island whose business had been to collect specimens of popular literature was on his return unable to say whether the islanders made use of rhyme.

Not less interesting than the songs are the prose pieces which Mr. Archer appends, particularly the match-making dialogues. It is well known that match-makers in primitive societies very seldom approach the subject of their visit in direct terms. Some examples of the round-about and allusive methods of match-makers have been given in books on Africa; but I have met with no specimens so highly developed as those given by Mr. Archer. The Uraons throw themselves into the business of ritual allegory with an unstinting zest. The idea that it is not genteel to embark upon a matter of business without fictitious preliminaries is widely spread. It still survives in old-fashioned Chinese and Japanese letters, in which a long preamble about the recipient's "health and vigour" being successfully maintained "despite the increasing severity of the weather" invariably precedes the equally obligatory "what I wanted to say is as follows". Such preliminaries bear no relation either to the recipient's actual state of health, or to the actual state of the weather.

The Uraon riddles which Mr. Archer gives have the great advantage of being on the whole fairly easy. I have very seldom before been able to guess a riddle of any kind, whether European or Asiatic. But I guessed "A white umbrella stands in a field" (Answer: "the mushroom") without the slightest difficulty.

ARTHUR WALEY

# PREFACE

ALMOST all the poems and marriage material translated in this book were collected in the Gumla subdivision of the district of Ranchi in Chota Nagpur, India, while I was subdivisional officer there from 1934 to 1937. About a third of the riddles were collected in the Jashpur *thana* of the Jashpur State in 1938, a quarter in the *Sadr* subdivision of Ranchi, and the remainder in Gumla later in the same year. Poems 9, 38, 40, 43, 44, 46, 57, 64 and 65 are translations of Poems 40 (p. 80), 10 (p. 95), 11 (p. 95), 15 (p. 96), 1 (p. 96), 18 (p. 97), 14 (p. 104), 51 (p. 89) and 17 (p. 84) respectively in Hahn's *Khurukh* Folk-lore from a collection made in Lohardaga *thana* of Ranchi District about the year 1900.

In most cases the language of the originals is Uraon, but in parts of Gumla subdivision the Uraons now speak a debased mixture of Uraon and Hindi, and in the poems which come from these parts the language of the originals is also mixed. This does not mean that such poems are any the less Uraon products, but only that linguistically certain originals are less purely Uraon than others.

It will be noticed that certain authorities spell Uraon as "Oraon". Both are possible versions, but I have preferred the former as it is on the whole in greater contemporary use.

Unlike the English social system in which one could pass one's life without coming into contact with poetry, the Uraon tribal system uses poetry as a vital appendix to dancing, marriages, and the cultivation of a crop—functions in which all Uraons join as part of their tribal life. Apart from these functions there is no Uraon poetry, and without this poetry the functions are incomplete. It follows that a dance poem and a marriage poem are as much the equipment of an Uraon as his axe and his plough. He would as little dream of going to a wedding or a dance and not using them or of using them apart from their contexts as he would of going to plough without his bullocks or of taking his plough with him for fishing. This is the reason for the classes in which the poems are grouped—classes which follow faithfully Uraon grouping. And it is also the reason why a collection of Uraon poems needs to include some analysis of Uraon marriages and dancing. Without such an analysis, Uraon poetry is not fully understood.

My thanks are due to B. Jugeshwari Prasad and the following Uraons—Chotan Ram, Ramprem Bhagat, Kinu Bhagat, Champa Bhagat, Martin Minj, Litungu Bhagat, and Jauru Bhagat—for help in the collection of the poems; to Mr. Mansidh Kujur and Miss Mariam Kanswar for aid in collecting riddles; to Mr. H. J. B. Le Patourel, Superintendent, Jashpur State, for enthusiastic help during my tour of the State in 1938; to Mr. Edward Kujur for assistance in the translation of certain poems; and to B. Sankta Prasad for help in collecting and translating certain Ahir poems.

My special thanks are due to B. Bishram Trofimus Toppo for continuous help in inquiries and translation; to Mr. Alan Bartlett and Mr. J. Bronowski, both of whom read the manuscript and made important suggestions; and to Miss Beryl de Zoete for advice on dance terms. Above all, from Mildred Archer, I had the stimulus of an equal enthusiasm for the Uraons and much practical help; and from Mr. Arthur Waley, I have received not only encouragement and a preface but the great kindness of seeing the book through the press, after I had been recalled to India.

Versions of certain poems, the marriage sermon and a dialogue have appeared in *New Verse*, *Contemporary Poetry and Prose*, and *The Listener*, and to the editors of these papers I offer grateful acknowledgments.

# CONTENTS

# INTRODUCTION

# INTRODUCTION

## THE URAONS

The Uraons are an aboriginal tribe of Dravidian stock concentrated in the western half of Chota Nagpur in Central India.

According to their legends, an early home of the tribe was Rohtas, a small tableland which juts out of the Taimur hills in the Shahabad district of Bihar. But before they occupied this area the Uraons had probably come from a point in the Deccan and had moved up the River Narbadda and crossed the Vindhyas. For some centuries Rohtas acted as a tribal capital, but it eventually fell to Hindu invaders and the Uraons were forced out of this region into a zone in Chota Nagpur a hundred miles to the south-east. In the legends the period at Rohtas is the golden age of the tribe and Rohtas shines as a symbol of a heroic stability.

With the move into Chota Nagpur the tribe came into contact with two other aboriginal tribes—the Kharias and the Mundas—and for some time lived parallel to them, sharing in the work of opening up the jungle, clearing the hill-tops and preparing terraces of riceland in the ravines and valleys. This was followed by a gradual dissolution into separate areas—the Mundas concentrating in an area further east, while the Kharias went to the south-east. At an early stage the three tribes had elected a common over-raja for the purpose of defence, financing him by a system of small village payments.

Owing to the thickly forested character of the country, this over-raja can have had very few functions. The jungle in which the tribe made its home was an effective barrier to the outsider, and it was only in the sixteenth century that the expansion of Muhammedan power in Bihar threatened this isolation and undermined the security of the tribe. The threat was averted not by a tribal army but by tribute, and the history of the succeeding centuries is the history of a process by which increasing tribute coupled with a wish for wealth converted the over-raja into a landlord, destroyed the village ownership of land, and made the village headmen the servants of an imported landlord class. With the nineteenth and twentieth centuries, the development of roads, the shrinkage of the jungle, the diffusion of British administration, and the arrival of missionaries completed the breakdown of a world in which the Uraon, the Munda, and the Kharia brothers had formed the single triangle.

At the present day the Uraons are massed in southern Palamau, the northern and western parts of Ranchi district, and the eastern halves of the Native States of Sarguja and Jashpur in sufficient density to make this region an almost solidly Uraon area. Other groups are scattered in Singhbhum, Hazaribagh, and Gaya districts, and in the Native States of Bonai and Gangpur. As a result of emigration to the tea gardens there is also an Uraon "empire" in Assam and a few migrant colonies are strung out throughout North Bihar.

The main area consists of undulating country with descending terraces of ricefields and sweeping uplands marked with scattered trees and occasional mango groves. In places black boulders and small globular hills rise out of the reddish-brown soil, while to the north and west the jungle comes down in rolling hills. The winter is cold and sunny, while the dry heat of the summer turns to mild and cool weather in the rains.

Owing to the shrinkage of the jungle, the tribal routine is now almost entirely based on the rice crop, there is scarcely any hunting, and in its economic condition the tribe now approximates to the cultivator class in the rest of Bihar. There has, however, been very little weakening in the tribal sense of solidarity, and an Uraon village remains intensely and proudly Uraon. Similarly there have been very few radical changes in custom, and the Uraon villager, unless he is a convert to Christianity, still follows a routine of life based on the system of his ancestors. This system includes traditional rites for birth, marriage and death, two major festivals for accelerating the harvest, and a religion which sees the landscape in the light of a precise but scattered animism. Besides this framework and affording the village recurrent enjoyment is a scheme of tribal dancing and a body of tribal poems, riddles and dialogues into which the Uraon temperament has projected the excess energy of the tribe. These art forms remain rooted in the village routine, and in spite of the tribe's exposure to alien influences, dancing and singing persist as vital habits among the Uraons.

A few notes should be added on Uraon "character". To the earliest observers a capacity for cheerful hard work was the most notable characteristic of Uraons; and a sturdy gaiety, an exultation in bodily physique and a sense of fun are still their most obvious qualities. These are linked to a fundamental simplicity—a tendency to see an emotion as an action, and not to complicate it by postponement or cogitation. An Uraon hardly ever thinks about himself, and for this reason a state of anger is only with difficulty distinguished from an act of assault. In a similar way Uraons dislike doing nothing, and this perhaps explains both the frequency of their dancing and the round of visiting which occurs in the slack season of the year. Equally an Uraon dislikes being alone and he relishes a happy domestic life with a jolly wife, three or four children and a dog. Markets, marriages and liquor shops are also very popular because they bring Uraons together. The final picture is of a kindly simplicity and a smiling energy.

## URAON DANCES

For the Uraons dancing is essentially a village amusement. In a few dances, such as the blessing dance at weddings,[1] and the *Domkach* and *Matha* dances, only the women dance. But these are the exceptions, and in the majority of Uraon dances all the younger men and women participate. The village assembles all its "under-thirties" and they revolve through the night tossing and surging like a single unit in the circular rhythms. Occasionally boys and girls from other villages join

[1] See S. C. Roy, *The Oraons*, p. 298.

the dances; and at the *jatras* a group of villages joins forces in a mass dance. But for the purpose of the nightly dancing which goes on throughout the year each village is its own unit, and the village is the basis of the dance.

The dances fall into the following groups:

1. "Festival" dances for the following festivals:
   (*a*) *Phagua* and *Sarhul.*
   (*b*) *Karam.*

2. "*Jatra*" dances at the meetings of groups of villages:
   (*a*) *Jatra* (or *Khariah*).
   (*b*) *Jatra Lujhri* (= *Jhumair*).
   (*c*) *Chirdi* (= *Jeth Jatra*).

3. "Transitional" social dances which are danced between the periods of the "festival" dances or as substitutes for them:

| | |
|---|---|
| (*a*) *Matha*<br>(*b*) *Jadura*<br>(*c*) *Domkach* | between *Karam* and *Sarhul.* |
| (*d*) *Dhuriya*<br>(*e*) *Angani* | between *Sarhul* and the *Jeth Jatra.* |

4. Marriage dances which include:
   (*a*) The blessing dance.
   (*b*) The marriage *domkach.*

There are no essential differences of style between these four groups, and the fact that the "religious" dances overlap the festivals by sometimes several months suggests that they have no special religious meaning. A "festival" dance uses the same movements as a social dance, and a social dance uses the same framework as a "festival" dance. There are no special religious gestures, and it is rather that a dance-form is included in a festival as part of the general gaiety than that the festival imposes a form on the dance.

The movement of all the dances is circular. In the *Sarhul*

and *Karam* dances the dancers are as it were on the rim of an imaginary circle, and their lines move round it either swinging to and from the centre and making ground by a sideways drift, or going along the rim in file.

In the *Dhuriya* dance the rows of dancers radiate from the centre and the action is like a great turning fan. In all except the *Jatra* dances the drummers form the pivot of the dance, either swinging with their drums in the centre of the circle or slightly preceding the lines as they revolve round it.

The force of the dance style comes from the fact that each dance sets up its own mobile pattern—a pattern which affects one as if it were a vital machine. It does this by interlocking all the dancers into several compact lines so that each line swings and tosses as a single unit; and also by basing each dance on a set of four or eight extremely simple leg movements. The legs become swaying cylinders on to which the formal rhythms are imposed, while the torsos act as a rigid line to which the rhythm of the legs is attached. Occasionally the arms are used as additional cylinders to supplement the movements of the legs. In none of the dances is any importance attached to the toes or fingers or to any details of the body except in so far as they help to compose it as a simple geometric unit. The dance then consists of the simultaneous execution of these steps by each of the dancers—one set being used to start the lines moving anti-clockwise and a slightly varied set being used to bring it back in reverse. Each pattern of movement is repeated over and over again until the dance stops. On this basis the dance becomes a system of parallel poses, of simple organized limbs operating to the rhythmic din of the drums.

The speed of the dancing varies from dance to dance and also from region to region. The *Domkach* for instance is more placid than the *Jatra* dance. Certain dances—the *Karam* and *Dhuriya*—have brisker variants known as *lujhkis* or *lujhris*, which are meant to be danced with a more rapid zest. Then again within a dance itself, as in the *Jatra Lujhri* or *Jhumair*, a wide fluctuation of speed can occur. The dance works up to a roaring tempo, the lines career round the circle in a violent rhythm and then slacken to a slow and placid swing. As between the sexes also variations of speed are noticeable. At Bhumtel in Jashpur the boys and girls dance with equal energy and poise, but at Mandar the style of the girls is neat and compact, while the boys provide a swinging and leaping descant. Within the limits of the tribal style each area dances as it likes.

In many primitive tribes dancing has either a sexual, magical or symbolic significance. Uraon dances, however, do not seem to have any purpose other than amusement. Certainly there is little to suggest a sexual motive. The dances have the mechanical precision of a piece of military drill; and the line of boys and girls is like a line of uniforms. Neither the steps nor the mass action are sexual in character, and the arms and legs are used merely for the execution of simple fluid patterns. Even when the drummers indulge in variations, the poses are acrobatic capers rather than sexual gestures. In this respect the dances are domestic and abstract when compared, for instance, with the *kaaro* dance of the Wachandi[1] or with the dances of the Bison-horn Marias of Bastar in which a man with mock genitals may run among the dancers.[2] There is similarly no

[1] "A dance is executed in the moonlight around a pit which is surrounded with shrubbery. The pit and the shrubbery represent the female organ, which they are made to resemble, while the spears swung by the men represent the male member. The men jump around, betraying their sexual excitement with the wildest and most passionate gestures, thrusting their spears in the pit."—Hodgkinson's report on Australia, 1845, quoted Ernst Grosse, *The Beginnings of Art*, p. 220.

[2] W. V. Grigson, *The Maria Gonds of Bastar*, p. 186.

attempt to wear a sexual costume. The clothes of the girls are always practical and consist usually of three pieces—a blouse, a piece of cloth to wrap round the waist and knees, and a third to put on the bust and shoulders. The cloth conceals rather than displays the body. Equally the boys' loincloth and wrap are designed only for utility, and even when buttock bells are worn they are used not for any sexual effects but to reinforce the rhythm. Egret's feathers in the girl's hair and occasionally a yak's tail at the boy's waist and a peacock's plume in the hand complete the list of dancing attire. If there is any sexual stimulus in Uraon dances, it is only in the tension which the dances produce, the excitement generated by the beat of the drums, the mass influence of a line of boys on a line of girls, and in the general stimulus of exercise.

In the same way it is scarcely possible to regard any of the dances as magical. Roy has suggested that one of the objects of the dances is the "pantomimic representation of such incidents in their own lives as excite intense feelings of pleasure" and that this representation becomes magical through the operation of sympathy.[1] The element of pantomime, however, is very slight. In the *Karam* dance it is possible to detect a resemblance in the stooping poses and swaying arms to the cutting of paddy; and in the *Kesari* version[2] of the *Karam* dance, where the girls squat and thump the ground, their actions are said to mimic those of *kesari* gatherers. But in none of the other dances are the gestures descriptive or imitative; and even in the *Karam* dances, it is I think more a case of certain "work" movements being utilized as the basis of a dance-form than the object of the dance being to mimic the work. None of the Uraons whom I questioned about the dances suggested that they were magical or were intended to induce a magical result.

Equally it appears to be straining interpretation to regard any of the dances as symbolic. Roy states that the *Jadura* dances symbolize the desire for union and gives the ground that the separate lines of boys and girls back and advance together. He

[1] S. C. Roy, *The Oraons*, p. 275. [2] *Ibid.*, p. 296.

also states that the *Jatra* dances "appear to symbolize the bliss of wedded love" because the men and women dance in mixed lines. He goes on to suggest that these *Jatra* dances at the same time give "a pantomimic representation of hunting," arguing this from the fact that the men carry clubs and sticks and use a column formation. The same dance on its later appearance in the year's programme (*Chirdi Jatra*) is interpreted as symbolizing hunting and reaping. "As men and women join hands in the reaping operations, so do they dance together in one and the same row in the *Chirdi* dances." The *Jatra* dance would thus be a cross between a marriage and a hunt in the earlier part of the year and a cross between a hunt and a harvest in the later part. Similarly, "*Karam* dances are rude representations of the occupation of the people. As in their work in the fields so in their dances during this season the men and women are not intermixed but are arranged in separate groups."[1]

It is obvious that all these "symbols" are extremely vague and elastic; and none of them have any very urgent relation to Uraon life. A symbol is only a symbol if its range of reference is fairly precise; and when it has a degree of ambiguity, it is necessary that all the levels of meaning should reinforce each other. An aspect of a dance which can at one time be interpreted as a symbol of wedded love and at another as an act of harvesting is obviously too general to have symbolic power. It should be added also that the mere presence of clubs in a *jatra* obviously does not make a dance a hunt. As *jatra* dances are group dances of several villages where quarrels are not infrequent, a weapon is more likely to be for defence than for symbolism. And the reason why the women dance with the men of their own village at *jatras* is simply that they shall not be mixed up in other villages and separated from them. Other groupings of the sexes appear to be only periodic adjustments for varying the dances and avoiding monotony.[2]

[1] S. C. Roy, *The Oraons*, pp. 273–301.

[2] See also Appendix II.

## A CALENDAR OF URAON DANCES

The following calendar shows the approximate periods at which the various dances occur in the three areas of Mandar, Gumla and Jashpur *thanas*.

| *English Month* | *Uraon Month* | *Areas* | | |
|---|---|---|---|---|
| | | *1. Mandar* | *2. Gumla* | *3. Jashpur* |
| January–February | Magh | Jadura | Sarhul | Domkach |
| February–March | Phagun | Jadura<br>Marriage | Sarhul<br>Marriage | Sarhul<br>Domkach<br>Marriage |
| March–April | Chait | Marriage | Sarhul<br>Marriage | Sarhul<br>Domkach<br>Marriage |
| April–May | Baisakh | — | Sarhul | Sarhul<br>Dhuriya |
| May–June | Jeth | Jatra | Sarhul Jatra | Sarhul<br>Dhuriya<br>Jatra |
| June–July | Asar | Dhuriya | Dhuriya | Karam |
| July–August | Sawan | Karam | Dhuriya | Karam<br>Angani |
| August–September | Bhado | Karam | Karam | Karam<br>Angani |
| September–October | Asin | Jatra<br>Jatra lujhri<br>(jhumair) | Karam<br>Jatra (chirdi) | Karam<br>Jatra |
| October–November | Kartik | Jatra<br>Jatra lujhri | Karam<br>Jatra (chirdi)<br>Matha | Karam<br>Jatra |
| November–December | Aghan | Matha<br>Angani | Jadura | — |
| December–January | Pus | Matha<br>Jadura | Jadura | — |

## URAON DANCE POEMS

Uraon dance poems are fitted to the drum rhythms and are sung by the boys and girls while the dances revolve. Most of them are poems of four lines. In the dances which have a definite advance and reverse action the first two lines are called the *or* or opening movement and the third and fourth lines are known as the *kirtana* or reverse. The *or* takes the lines of dancers anti-clockwise on the circle. After it has been repeated three or four times there is a stop or hitch in the dance and the movement is reversed—the line moving back clockwise, while the *kirtana* is sung and repeated. Where there are more than four lines in the dance poem, the fifth and sixth lines and the seventh and eighth are treated as additional *kirtanas*, and after each *kirtana* has been sung and repeated the dance moves back into the *or* action and repeats the first two lines before it goes on to the next. A few dances do not have any obvious reverse action, and in these cases the *kirtana* is sung as an addition or variation to the *or*—the poem being sung over and over again for as long as the dance lasts.

All dance poems are classified in terms of the dances to which they belong—the dances having their own set of dance poems and also their own tunes. Since there are no major differences of form or content between the groups, a poem is always identified by its tune and not by any other method. A *Sarhul* dance poem, for instance, is simply a poem which is sung to a *Sarhul* tune. A *Karam* poem is a poem which is sung to a *Karam* tune. None of these tunes or poems is interchangeable and a poem of one group is never sung to the tune of another. The poem is rigidly attached to its tune and the tune is rigidly attached to its dance.

Almost all the poems are ancestral and are the result of a process of oral tradition working on a basis of group composition. Possibly a process of reconditioning goes on in the tribe and possibly a few new poems result every year from the festivals and *jatras*. But there is no poet class, and in so far as there is an effort by the tribe, it is invariably towards stability, the repetition of previous forms and not their extension. There is nowhere any wish to invent, and if a new poem is made it is the accidental result of the excitement of a dance or a chance offshoot from a previous poem. A new poem happens rather than is made.[1]

The dependence of the poems on certain fixed tunes might be supposed to lead to a rigidity of form. Actually, however, the tunes are very elastic and poems of widely varying verbal rhythms are fitted to them, much as in European churches the varying verses of a psalm are fitted to the same tune. A wide range of rhythmic variation is in fact characteristic of Uraon poems. There is no scale of feet or rhymes to which the poems are made to conform. Rhyme may occur but assonance is more usual, and the poems set up their own rhythms rather than follow any standard or stock base.

As a result of the clear division of many dances into the advance and the reverse, Uraon dance poems are not infrequently constructed in terms of a question and answer—the question balancing the advance while the answer follows the reverse.

"Crow, where are you coming from
With all your glossy feathers falling?"

"Which is the country whose girl has pigeon's feathers?"

"Whose is the red flag which the dew is wetting?"

[1] Compare Robert Graves, *The English Ballad*, pp. 12–13: "Anonymity in the present structure of society usually implies that the author is ashamed of his authorship or afraid of the consequences if he reveals himself; but in a primitive society is due just to carelessness of the author's name. This carelessness may be only on the part of the community; but in conditions where the poet-musician has not yet become a person of great distinction it is also on the part of the author. For there must be some original author who in the intoxication of fellowship starts the ballad going and even orders its general direction, but the peculiarity of communal composition is that this original author is merely acting as spokesman for the group and when the ballad is complete will not claim it as his own. The ballad is important, the group is important, but the individual counts for little." This description would apply to the composition of Uraon dance poems.

And where the poem is not in this form, it often implies a question—when, where, who, which, or even why. In the following poem, for example, there is no question but the last two lines answer one.

> "Your mother, girl
> Keeps you like a *koel*[1]
> For the young men, girl
> She keeps you like a *koel*."

Similar to this is the use of the command and compliance and the request and refusal.

> "Come closer, girl
> The shining girl is coming."
>
> "Come, girl, I say
> Come later, juri, she says."

Compare a similar method in English ballads:

> "Who killed cock robin?
> I said the sparrow
> With my bow and arrow
> I killed cock robin."

When questioned about the meaning of their poems, Uraons usually say that a poem is a poem and imply that it does not necessarily have a logical meaning. Dance poems are in fact regarded as parallel to dances—that is, as forms of excess energy, as art forms which do not necessarily refer to other parts of the village routine but have their own standards of validity. This does not prevent certain poems from being realistic and transcribing incidents of village life, but it explains the greater number which are concerned with different levels of image action.

Of the realistic poems a few are moral:

[1] See note to Poem 11.

"The diamond will it last?
Will the woman keep for you?"

A larger number are "joking" poems—poems by one sex about the other, poems about mock love-making, leg-pulling, anecdotes. Compare the insects in the figs (60), the falling nuts (76), the wife and the drum (40), the threatening girls (38 and 84)' and the *Karam* poems about love proposals.

"If you get a daughter, she will call you mother
If you get a son, he will call me father."

The majority of dance poems, however, do not so much serve a dominant emotion as project a set of images. At its simplest the image parallels a line of action which Uraons enjoy in their daily life.

"I put on my tattered clothes
And went to catch fish."

Here it refers to an already existing interest; and the interest explains the poem. Very similar are poems in which the image is a natural object which the Uraons like:

"The palms toss, the palms shake."
"The pretty parrot stays in the grove."

The recollection of the object with its visual stimulus becomes the end of the poem. More complicated but on the same level are poems in which two images of natural facts are intensified by impinging on each other:

"On a kend pole a *dhichua*[1] sits
In the paddy fields a parrot swoops and wheels."

Here the force is partly in the natural facts and partly in the contrast of the actions. The poem acts as a focus of the images. Compare the poem

"The mango tree is withered by the frost
The feathers of the parrot fall"

[1] See note to Poem 68.

where the withering of the mango is equated with the falling of the feathers and the force is in the similarity of the action. Similarly in the poem

> "Come and visit us, brother
> With your diamond girl
> In the morning, brother
> With your diamond girl"

the force is n the simultaneous suspension of certain natural images—"morning," "diamond" and "girl" and their mutual fusion, "diamond" linking "girl" with "morning." In all these cases the images are literal; that is, they parallel natural facts, their connections refer to ordinary events, and the explanation of the poems is the interest attaching to the action or the object in ordinary life.

In other poems, however, all equivalence or value in ordinary life is abandoned and the images work through their strangeness. Compare

> "Brother, your bangles
> Have fallen in the water, are in the water"

> "Whose is the blue grove which the *koels* are filling?"

> "The son of the raja brought the thin cloth
> In the cold, the cold
> In the heat, the heat"[1]

and the long *Karam* poem (28) where there is a developed use of irrational connections.

In a book on Surrealism, Mr. Herbert Read writes: "two realities . . . cohere as an image and gain their emotive power from the presence in the unconscious of a hidden connecting link. There is no need, in any poetic analysis, to reveal that

[1] Compare:

> "On the first day of Christmas
> My true love sent to me
> A partridge in a pear tree."

repressed connection; the poetic reality lies in the evident power of the image and is no stronger—indeed, may be much weaker—if its latent meaning is made manifest."[1]

Among the Uraons the actions of dancing and singing both operate to free the poems from a dependence on the normal. Singing, by providing a different form from ordinary speech, enables abnormal images to be used without a sense of oddness; while dancing sets up a tension which acts as a trigger to the unconscious. In these circumstances unusual images can at once be created and accepted. At the same time the amusement and exhilaration which the dances create put a premium on certain types of poem—"joking" poems which add to the amusement and poems which add to the exhilaration. For the latter poems with a message, a moral or an attitude would be out of key, and the best type is the poem which projects an image. These images by their *evident power* add to the exhilaration.

In England, where dancing is personal and not collective,

"Heaven is in your arms, my dear"

jazz songs are usually sentimental. Here also the act of dancing undermines the sense of what is normal, but instead of resulting in vivid images it merely supports a romantic escape.

"Now that our love is spoken
Now that I know you're mine
Gone is the gloom and shadow
And life is just divine
Stay in my heart for ever . . ."

In this contrast lies the difference of two poetic traditions and two cultures.

[1] Herbert Read, *Surrealism*, p. 77.

# URAON DANCE POEMS

# PHAGUA AND SARHUL

For the purpose of dancing the *Phagua* and *Sarhul* festivals are regarded as extensions of each other—the same dance-forms being used throughout the period and, except when they refer to a festival, the same dance poems being used for both.

The *Phagua* festival occurs in March and is the Uraon equivalent of New Year's Eve—seeing out the old year and bringing in the New. It marks the end of the marriage season and the period of relaxation after the harvest.

The ritual consists of setting up some branches of the cotton tree, wrapping them in straw and offering some country bread and incense to them. The branches are then burnt and the festival ends in dancing and drinking.

The *Sarhul* festival comes a month later and has a double significance. In one aspect it is a "vegetation" ceremony—an act of rejoicing in the jungle which has already come into flower. In the other it is a "fecundity" ceremony—a marriage of the earth with the sun on the assumption that the soil is ready to be quickened. The fertility of the jungle is used, as it were, to stimulate the fertility of the fields. From one point of view, therefore, the appearance of blossom on the *sal* trees is an indispensable prerequisite of the festival.[1] From the other an indispensable preliminary is that the ploughed fields should be left bare to the sun for a month prior to the festival. Finally, the element of rejoicing involves drinking and dancing, while the fecundity aspect is seen in the mimic marriage of the earth and the sun.

The ritual commences with ceremonial baths by the men and women and the stacking of some selected rice in winnowing baskets. A grindstone is then put in the courtyard of the house of the *pahan* or village priest and on it are placed

[1] Roy has pointed out that *sal* branches by reason of their heavy blossom are naturally associated with fertility.

three bundles of straw and a yoke. The *pahan* and his wife sit on the yoke while the *pahan's* assistant, the *pujari*, with his wife sit to their right. A mimic marriage is then gone through —the *pahan* representing the sun and his wife the earth, while the *mahto* or village headman officiates by putting oil and scarlet powder on their heads. Rice beer is then offered by the headman to the village ancestors, and later some of the stacked rice is sanctified by the priest and put aside for use at sowing. There is then a procession to the village *sarna* or sacred grove, where fowls are sacrificed to the village ghosts and to the Sun God. The Sun God is asked to bless the *Sarhul* and make it merry and to grant prosperity to the village in the coming year. The *pahan* then returns to his house for a ceremonial drenching, and after that there is a men's feast in the grove composed of rice and the sacrificial fowls. This is followed by a women's feast in the *pahan's* house, and the night passes in general drinking and dancing.[1]

The festival has for the Uraons the gladness of Easter Day— an exultation in the brilliant weather and the flowering trees, and the sense of sprouting life.

1 BAMBOO hill is burning down
And the clouds thunder
The men are hunting
And the clouds thunder.

Usually the weather in March and April is sultry and jungle fires are not uncommon. The hunt referred to is the *Phagu shikar* or Spring hunt, which until the present century was in many areas a vital ceremony. Of recent years the decline in the area under jungle and the scarcity of animals have combined to make it a piece of hollow play; and in many villages it has been abandoned.

[1] S. C. Roy, *Oraon Religion and Customs*, pp. 193–227.

2 Crow, where are you coming from
With all your glossy feathers falling?
Crow, coming from the east
With all your glossy feathers falling.

3 *Juri*, leave me
My clothes are coming down
Are coming down
Let them come down, *juri*
Let them come down
We will dance the *bheja* naked
We will dance the *bheja* naked.

The *bheja* is any dance in which the men and women form a mixed line—a boy having a girl on either arm, a girl having a boy on either arm. The poem illustrates the Uraon view of what is "daring"—the semi-naughty proposal which sends Uraon girls into shrieks of laughter.

"*Juri*" is a term which may cover a boy-boy, boy-girl, or girl-girl relationship. It means a pair of young persons, similar in looks, age or height—a boy's boy-friend or girl-friend, a girl's girl-friend or boy-friend. Very frequently there is nothing in the poem to show which relationship is meant, and even the balance of probability is not obvious. Almost all Uraon girls have their particular girl-friends, and the attachment means as much to them as an interest in a boy. Consequently a poem which looks as if it means an invitation from a boy to a girl very often only means a girl inviting a girl.

4 Come and visit us, brother
With your diamond girl
In the morning, brother
With your diamond girl.

There is no proof that diamonds were ever found in Chota Nagpur, but there is a Mughal legend that they used to come from this area. The Uraons use "diamond" as a stock image for the brilliant and the precious, and a very common use is as an epithet for Chota Nagpur itself. This image is conventional but it continues to be vital, and the phrase—"this diamond Chota Nagpur"—summarizes the flashing landscape, the clarity of the weather and the passion of Uraons for their native land.

"Brother", "sister", "father", "mother". The use of these terms by Uraons is analogous to what L. H. Morgan has called the "classifying" system of certain Australian tribes. Freud in *Totem and Taboo* explains this system as meaning "that a man calls not only his begetter 'father' but also every other man who according to the tribal regulations might have married his mother and thus become his father; he calls "mother" not only the woman who bore him but also every other woman who might have become his mother without violation of the tribal laws; he calls 'brothers' and 'sisters' not only the children of all the persons named who stand in the parental group relation with him, and so on. The kinship names . . . do not therefore necessarily point to a blood relationship; they signify much more the social than the physical relations." Freud adds: "An approach to this classifying system is perhaps to be found in our nursery, when the child is induced to greet every male and female friend of the parents as 'uncle' and 'aunt,' or it may be found in a transferred sense when we speak of 'brothers of Apollo' or 'sisters in Christ.'

5 SCARLET for half a pice, mother
Scarlet adorns the head
Anklets for five rupees, mother
Anklets adorn the legs.

Scarlet is the powder used for dabbing the forehead as a mark of marriage. The scarlet enhances the beauty of the head in the same sense that marriage completes a girl. In one poem there is a catalogue of the parts of the body with the objects which particularly adorn them—a necklace the neck, bangles the arm, anklets the legs, and so on. The idea is that one object is a complement of another, the means by which an object is seen at its best. In the marriage poems the idea is constantly used. "The nest of the white ant is graced by the cobra." The boy is the "life" of the village. The girl is the "life" of the family. The family is enhanced by the girl. The girl is enhanced by her husband.

6 MOTHER, the ripe figs
Fall without notice
In the midnight, mother
Fall without notice.

7 THE deer barks in the four quarters of the night
Jungle boy, where is the abandoned calf?
The infant calf
Jungle boy, where is the abandoned calf?

8 LOOK, girl, the *sarhul* moon
Rises like a straw umbrella
Look, girl, in the morning
It rises like a straw umbrella.

In this poem and the next the third line utilizes a common stock variant for constructing the *kirtana*—"*pairi biri*"—in the morning. In a poem such as No. 4 the use merely connects an image with the time of day normal for it, but in others such as the present poem the use results in a distortion. The use is explicable either on the ground that the poem was made in strictly traditional terms, that is, without a stimulus from or a reference to nature, and was artificial because there was no particular need for it to be natural; or on the ground that the tension of the dancing during which the poem was made stimulates "a willing suspension of disbelief," makes every poem to some extent "abstract" and brings into operation the fancies of the unconscious. In the latter view the traditional would fuse with the irrational. The irrational would find the stock variant to hand and would use it.

9 THE jungle withers
To a road for the girls
In the morning withers
To a road for the girls.

10 WHOSE is the blue grove where the *koels* are going?
It is the blue grove of the raja which the *koels* are filling.[1]

11 YOUR mother, girl
Keeps you like a *koel*
For the young men, girl
She keeps you like a *koel*.

For the Uraons the *koel* or Indian cuckoo is in a class by itself, and one of their poems permits a boy to catapult all other birds, but admonishes him on no account to kill a *koel*. For this reason the grove which the *koels* fill in the preceding

[1] For "blue", see the note to Poem 152.

poem inevitably belongs to a raja; and for the same reason the *koel* is used as a symbol for an object of value and affection. Compare its use in Poem 158.

12 NEAR the spring is a life-and-death tree
Throw stones, *juri*, and I will catch the flowers
If you throw stones and get me the flowers
I will let you dance the *bheja* with me.

A *gulaichi* or life-and-death tree—a member of the magnolia family—is usually planted by the little shed to Devi Mai, the earth mother, which is found in every Uraon village. It has a white velvety blossom which merges into yellow at the centre. It is called the life-and-death tree from the bare and bleak arms out of which the blossom sprouts. Its leaves, which in some respects resemble the laurel's, appear when the flowers are withering.

13 Why, Parbatia
Why go to Bhutan?
Look at the changes in the country
The new jail in Ranchi.

Parbatia—a girl's name.

The Uraon drift to the tea gardens of Assam and Bhutan—the Himalayan foothills to the north-east of Bihar—commenced towards the end of the nineteenth century and was facilitated by the pressure of a growing population on the land, exploitation by the landlords, and indirect coercion by the recruiting agents of the tea gardens. The Uraons have now "colonized" this Himalayan tract and as a result of greatly improved conditions many families have permanently settled there. The standard of living is slightly but perceptibly higher than in Chota Nagpur, and ready money in the form of wages from the gardens is made more easily than at home. For this reason the tea gardens have now become a kind of insurance against famine and the effects of a large family; and many Uraons migrate from Ranchi for short periods, save a little money, and then return.

14 BEFORE the windows and the doors
Lakho Mahto rides his horse
Winner of renown in the raja's house
Before the windows and the doors
Lakho Mahto rides his horse.

I have been unable to find out who Lakho Mahto, Durgan Sai (Poem 50) and Raja Dillip Nath Sai (Poem 69) were. They were presumably local heroes or even magnates who for a time caught the imagination.

# KARAM

THE *Karam* festival occurs in August at the climax of the monsoon when the paddy is standing in the fields but has not yet come into ear. It marks a period of relaxation between the arduous work of transplanting the paddy and the rigours of the harvest; and is possibly a "fecundity" festival to help the ripening of the crop.

The centre of the ritual consists in the cutting of three branches of a *Karam* tree and their installation in the akhra or dancing ground. The branches are called the "*Karam Raja*". The entry of the branches into the village is accompanied by dancing, and after the installation *Karam* dances revolve round the Raja through the night. The following morning the branches are garlanded and the *Karam* legend is recited. Flowers are then thrown over the Raja and offerings of curds and rice are made. Red *Karam* baskets full of grain are also put before the branches, and some ceremonially nurtured barley seedlings are distributed among the boys and girls who put the yellow blades in their hair. The blessing of the *Karam* Raja is then sought and the branches are taken up and carried by women through the village. A halt is made at the houses of the village *pahan* and *mahto*, the Uraon religious and secular heads, and at each house the branches are anointed with the oil and scarlet powder which are part of the apparatus of a marriage. The branches are then thrown in a stream.[1]

With its *Karam* Raja and *Karam* tree the festival has obvious affinities with Christmas.

[1] S. C. Roy, *Oraon Religion and Customs*, pp. 240–247.

15 RAJA, you made an *akhra* at a far-off place
And planted the *Karam* in the middle of the village
They have taken the *Karam* to a distant place
Your *akhra* is deserted.

An *akhra* is a square, usually twenty to thirty yards wide and usually with houses adjoining it and a spreading tree under which the dancers can rest. It acts as the village dancing floor.

"Raja" is not necessarily the Raja of Chota Nagpur or the Raja of a Native State. The term is used to include the Uraon leader of a group of villages, the man who rides on a totem at a *jatra*, and even, with a kind of mock magnificence, a bridegroom.

16 THE *Karam* is coming
Shaking its branches
Shaking shaking
Shaking shaking
Mother it comes
To ask for the oil
To ask for the scarlet
To ask for the oil
To ask for the scarlet.

17 Below the *Karam* the girl sits
She tends the *Karam*
She tends the *Karam*
Of mud is the drum
Of copper are the cymbals
Listen my mother
Listen my father.

The drum of this poem is the *mandar*—a cylindrical drum with a skin top and mud sides. Drums and cymbals are used for dancing to.[1]

[1] For an analysis of Uraon musical instruments, see S. C. Roy, *The Oraons*, pp. 180–184.

18 *Karam Karam* O *Karam* Raja
For you O *Karam* is a royal umbrella
Give us O *Karam* rice and riches
Give us O *Karam* sweets and cattle
For you O *Karam* is a royal umbrella.

19 The *Karam* is going
The *Karam* is going
The *Karam* is going to leave us now
Give the oil
Give the scarlet
Bid goodbye to *Karam*
The *Karam* is wanting
Rice in the basket
Money in the wall
The *Karam* demands its toll.

*Karam* poems include *puja* or worship poems about the *Karam* Raja, such as the four preceding; but like the dance poems of other festivals, the majority have no religious connections and are "*Karam*" only because they are sung to the *Karam* tune and are danced to during the *Karam* period.

20 WHOSE is the red flag which the dew is wetting?
It is the red flag of the rani which the dew is wetting.

"The red flag." Compare also Poems 28, 35, 100, 155 and 183. "Red", from its association with blood, is a symbol of vitality. Among many Hindu castes it is used as a blood substitute, and the shrines of deities to whom animal sacrifices are acceptable are covered with scarlet smears. For this reason it is considered a divine and therefore a lucky colour by many Hindus.[1] Possibly the practice of anointing the foreheads of

[1] R. V. Russell, *Tribes and Castes of the Central Provinces*, vol. iv, p. 107.

Uraon couples with scarlet powder is a substitute for the act of blood exchange—a practice which still exists in certain castes, as for instance the Tirhutia Musahars of Purnea District in Bihar. D. H. Lawrence in *Apocalypse* suggests that there has been a shift of colour symbols in different races and that the red dragon which was formerly a symbol of the vivifying potency of the world had become a symbol for its hostile and destructive activity by the time the *Apocalypse* was written. In India "red" appears to have been stable as a symbol of potent goodness.

21 WHO cut the flute on the small hill?
When the cattle left their grazing, the cowherd cut the flute.

22 WHICH is the bird that cries in the river?
Which is the bird that calls in the night?
It is the wild goose that cries in the river
It is the peacock that calls in the night.

23 IN the *Karam* river
The sand is thrashed by the water
The small fish
Glint in the stream.

24 WHO has brought the thin cloth
In the cold, the cold
In the heat, the heat?
The son of the raja brought the thin cloth
In the cold, the cold
In the heat, the heat.

25 THE tiger and the bear are ploughing
The dog scatters the seed
The bear and the monkey pull the seedlings
The black farmer ties the bundles
And the mouse breaks the string.

26 IN the swampy pastures
The small fishes are appearing
Mother, give me the bamboo sieve
And I will skim the water for the fishes.

A common sight during the rains is to see Uraons fishing in the paddy fields for the tiny fish which come in from the streams but which seem to spring from nowhere.

27 THE rain drizzles, the rain
Reaches to the verandah
Mother, give me a spice-coloured *dhoti*
And I will walk in the village.

A *dhoti* is the long piece of cloth, as distinct from the loincloth, in which Uraons swathe their legs.

28 FROM where are the black clouds rising?
Noise of the rain falling
Where is the rain falling?
In the east the clouds are massing
Noise of the rain falling
In the west the rain is falling
Whose is the red turban which the rain is wetting?
Noise of the rain falling
Whose is the long hair which the rain is wetting?
It is the red turban of the flirting boy which the rain is wetting
Noise of the rain falling

It is the long hair of the pale-skinned woman that
the rain is wetting
Where shall I dry the red turban?
Noise of the rain falling
Where shall I dry the long hair?
I shall dry the red turban on the dead bushes
Noise of the rain falling
I shall dry the long hair in the body's core
Choose the cloth and tie the red turban
Noise of the rain falling
Comb and tie the long hair.

29 THINK. What are your origins?
Where was your heart born?
You began in the cleared forest
You were born in the new lands
When disaster struck Rohtas
Then was your birth in Nagpur.

30 THE captive birds, the animals, the creatures
Write with their lips
The British rule
The court's judicial order
Write as they wish.

Mr. Arthur Waley, in his introduction to *The Temple and Other Poems*, says: "In China folk-songs were collected for political purposes. They were regarded as a means by which the governing classes could get into touch with the common people, could discover their grievances and aspirations." In England a similar function might nowadays be fulfilled by broadsheets. But among the Uraons scarcely any poems contain "information", and the present poem is almost the only Uraon poem which could be called "political".

31 LOOK at Ranchi town
Filling with soldiers
I see I see the white
Soldiers fill the streets.

32 IN the clear waters of Palkote
The scarlet held its colour
Sit, rani, and untie your *sari*
Dreams are of oil, dreams are of scarlet
Tell me the end of the fig's flower.

In this poem the references are sexual. In the first two lines the tenacity of the scarlet powder which is used as a mark of marriage is implied by its proof against dilution. "Untying the *sari*" is a preparation for a sexual act, while the desire for marriage shows itself in dreams of marriage apparatus—oil and scarlet powder. Finally a marriage ends in pregnancy as a flower ends in a fruit.

33 THE mat is stained with scarlet
Slowly you weep
Slowly you weep
Give courage to the petted girl
Slowly you weep
Slowly you weep.

In this poem also the allusion is to the scarlet marriage powder. "Weeping" refers to the sorrow of a girl at leaving her home after marriage.

34 JUNE and the human sacrificers stop me
July August and the rivers check me
Under the hills you married me, mother
From full eyes the tears drop.

Human sacrifices to the *Mahadana* spirit[1] used to be offered by Uraons, and even to-day it is doubtful if the practice is entirely extinct. The object of the practice is to restore fertility at times of famine or drought or, as in the present poem, in June if the rains are late. It is not, however, known if any ritual is connected with the observance—beyond killing a victim and throwing the head in a field; and in a murder case from Bassia *thana* in 1936 with which I had to deal this was all that could be ascertained. The extent of the fear may be judged from the fact that in the same year a death in Ghaghra *thana* which was finally attributed to lightning was believed by many to have been caused by human sacrificers. Among the Uraons the practice appears to have involved only secret murders (usually of old women) and does not seem to have required the breeding of a victim-class or any elaborate public ceremonies.

35 SON-IN-LAW, a small figure, mother
Comes holding a red gun
Daughter, your small son
Comes crying on the path.

In the poem the small son is an extension of the son-in-law. Similarly, the mother and daughter blend together and are not distinct. The combination of the gun with the crying child gives the poem a marriage reference—a gun being one of the spectacular articles carried in a wedding procession, while the crying child fills the role of the bridegroom. Compare the marriage poem (141), "The boy who must be married bitterly cries."

[1] See S. C. Roy, *Oraon Religion and Customs*, pp. 50–52.

36 MOTHER, from what country will you get me a bride?
From what country will you get me a bride?
Slowly slowly my boy
From Nagpur we shall get you a bride.

37 WHERE are you going, mother?
Your boy is going mad for want of a girl
The mother has prepared the rice and *dal*
The father has chosen a bride
I will come from Ranchi
And see that my son is married.

38 VISIT the village
But do not go to the girls
Do not go to the girls
In the girls' quarter
Is the noise of giggling
Do not go to the girls.

39 WHY do you spend this money?
The girl from Basua will not stay with you
Her own man
Waits for her with his own umbrella.

40 BUY a drum, Lalu brother
You will feel as if you have a wife
If the drum gets broken, Lalu brother
You will feel as if your wife has left you.

41 TAKE off your clothes and put them on the stool
Will you again run to Lohardaga?
Your *juri* fetches you
And you joke together all the way.

In this poem a mother addresses a daughter. The girl's object in running to Lohardaga is simply to be brought back by her boy-friend. The original makes it clear that *juri* is masculine.

42 GIRL, do not go to the spring beyond the village
Spread your mat and lie down easily with me
If you get a daughter, she will call you mother
If you get a son, he will call me father.

43 COME girl I say
It is muddy she answers
Come later, *juri*, she says
Come later
Lying we will lie
Sleeping we will sleep
Then we shall be happy.

44 IT is muddy you say, girl
Come later, *juri*, you say
I will spread a small cloth
I will wrap a big cloth
And hide you under an umbrella.

Compare the English nursery rhyme:

Little maid, pretty maid, whither goest thou?
Down in the forest to milk my cow.
Shall I go with thee? No, not now;
When I send for thee, then come thou.

45 IN an upper field, I said "Girl, please let me"
"No, brother, it will make me muddy
My clothes are like flowers, my life is like gold
No, brother, it will make me muddy."

The excuse that the girl's clothes will get spoilt if she lets her boy-friend have his way is a not uncommon device for hinting at the larger issue. Compare Robert Burns, "I'm owre young to marry yet":

"My mammie coft me a new gown,
The kirk maun hae the gracing o't;
Were I to lie wi' you, kind Sir,
I'm fear'd ye'd spoil the lacing o't"

and the following Ahir poem from Harihargunj *thana*, Palamau district, Bihar, which begins with a newly married boy and girl doubting if they will like each other and ends with the girl's excitement at her husband.

*Before and after going to bed*

"My father gave me my dress
And my father dyed it
Lie away from me, you fatherless boy
Or you will crumple it."

"My father gave me my turban
And my father dyed it
Lie away from me, you wanton girl
Or you will stain it with your scarlet."

"Had I known my husband was coming
I would have planted him a garden
Then you would have had shade to come in
And shade to go in

And your heart would have been calm
I would have tied my breasts in a black slip
And added bells to the ribbons
I would have washed my face with white earth
And piled my hair
I would have given a scarlet streak to the parting
With a whisker of barley."

46 LEAVE me leave me, *juri*
My arms are breaking
My arms are breaking
I will leave you, *juri*
But I shall not feel happy
I shall not feel happy.

In this poem *juri* might mean a girl addressed by a girl, but more probably the reference as in the four preceding poems is to a girl-boy relationship.

# JATRA

URAON *jatras* are meetings of a group of villages for a common dance. They occur from March-June (*sarhul jatras*) and from September to November (*Karam jatras*).

Roy gives the following explanation of their origin and function.

"Periodical meetings of neighbouring clans . . . came to be regularly held at convenient centres at the beginning of each changing season of the year, and helped in welding the various intermarrying clans into a regular tribe. It was at these *jatras* that the young men of the tribe came to choose their mates from amongst the girls of clans other than their own; it was there that outstanding disputes about game were settled; and it was then that the customary dances and songs of the outgoing season were formally exchanged for the dances and songs appropriate to the incoming season. And to this day it is at these *jatras* that new dances and songs are similarly taken up and disputes about game are settled by arbitration or by fight. Nor is it unusual to find, even to this day, attachments formed between young men and girls of different villages during these seasonal *jatras*, ending, if other considerations permit, in marriage." "In fact the *jatras* of old would seem to have been the great Social Congress of the Oraons—the first and the last attempt to secure and maintain the solidarity of the tribe." He also states that the *Jatra* dances have for one of their main objects the magical control or stimulation of nature for the benefit of the villages concerned—a group stimulus for an area as against a village stimulus for a village.[1]

In my own experience of Gumla and Mandar *thanas*, *jatras* are the equivalent of "socials" and do not appear to have any business function. A series of *jatras* is held in each area in each of the *jatra* seasons. In Mandar *thana*, for instance, June (or *jeth*) *jatras* are held in Dungri (three miles south-west of

[1] S. C. Roy, *The Oraons*, pp. 312–319.

Mandar itself), Burha Kurkra (two miles south), Katanga (five miles south-east), and Keskani (three miles east), while October (or *kartik*) *jatras* are held at Hesme (two miles west), Loheya (three miles south), and Murma (three miles east). Approximately the same villages go to the *jatras*. The reason for this duplication appears to be simply the mass excitement of the enormous crowds and the thrill of the dancing.

I have not been able to obtain any evidence of their function as a marriage agency. Roy states that "as there is a regular round of such dancing-meetings held one after another in several neighbouring villages, the young men and girls have repeated opportunities of coming together."[1] But there is not a great deal of inter-village mixing at a *jatra*. A village is in the crowd, but it keeps together as a group. And the Uraons from whom I inquired in Mandar *thana* did not know of any cases of boys marrying girls whom they had met at *jatras*. This would also appear to be the case in the Jashpur *thana* of Jashpur State, and it agrees with the impression I formed of Gumla subdivision during my stay there.

It is also not quite clear in what sense the object of a *jatra* is to make a *formal exchange* of songs and dances. A *jatra* has its own dance-form, and during the *jatra* seasons this is the only form of dance which is danced at *jatras*. But at the same time as the *jatra* seasons are on, non-*jatra* dances are danced in the villages. *Karam* dances, for instance, are continued in the villages in September and October, although *Chirdi jatra* dances are danced in the September *jatras*. There does not appear to be any connection between a *jatra* and a new dance.

For a description of a *jatra*, Dalton's vivid account, which I append, cannot easily be bettered.

"The flags of each village are brought out and set up on the road that leads to the place of meeting. This incites the young men and maidens to hurry through their morning work and look up their *jatra* dresses which are by no means ordinary attire. Those who have some miles to go put up their finery in a bundle to keep it fresh and clean, and proceed to some

[1] S. C. Roy, *The Oraons*, p. 313.

tank or stream in the vicinity of the tryst grove, and about two o'clock in the afternoon may be seen all around groups of girls laughingly making their toilettes in the open air, and young men in separate parties similarly employed. When they are ready, the drums are beaten, huge horns are blown, and thus summoned the group from each village forms its own procession. In front are young men with swords and shields or other weapons, the village standard bearers with their flags and boys waving yak's tails, or bearing poles with fantastic arrangements of garlands and wreaths intended to represent umbrellas of dignity. Sometimes a man riding on a wooden horse is carried horse and all by his friends as the raja, and others assume the form of, or paint themselves up to represent, certain beasts of prey. Behind this motley group the main body form compactly together as a close column of dancers in alternate ranks of boys and girls, and thus they enter the grove where the meeting is held in a cheery dashing style, wheeling and countermarching, and forming lines, circles and columns with grace and precision. The dance with these movements is called *Khariah*, and it is considered to be an Oraon rather than a Munda dance, though Munda girls join in it. When they enter the grove, the different groups join and dance the *Khariah* together forming one vast procession and then a monstrous circle. The drums and musical instruments are laid aside, and it is by their voices alone that the time is given; but as many hundreds, nay thousands join, the effect is grand. In serried ranks so closed up that they appear jammed, they circle round in file, all keeping perfect step, but at regular intervals the strain is terminated by a *hururu*, which reminds one of Paddy's 'huroosh' as he 'welts the floor,' and at the same moment they all face inwards and simultaneously jumping up come down on the ground with a resounding stamp that marks the finale of the movement, but only for a momentary pause. One voice with a startling yell takes up the strain again, a fresh start is made, and after gyrating thus till they tire of it, the ring breaks up, and separating into village groups they perform other dances independently till near sunset, then they all go dancing home."[1]

47 WHICH is the country whose girl has pigeon's feathers?
Which is the country whose girl has flowerless branches?
For the girl from Nagpur are the pigeon's feathers
For the girl from Barwe are the flowerless branches.

Barwe is the tract of country ringed in by the Netarhat plateau and the Kurumgarh hills and extending up to the River Sankh. The hills contain large blocks of jungle and the valleys are seamed with ravines. The Uraons live closer to the "hunger line" in Barwe than in other parts of Gumla subdivision.

Nagpur does not refer to the Nagpur of the Central Provinces, but is a shortened form of Chota Nagpur and means the Gumla-Lohardaga-Mandar area—the heart of the Uraon country in Ranchi district. The area has less jungle and is correspondingly more fertile than Barwe.

"Flowerless branches" are symbols of infertility. For "pigeon", compare Poem 112.

48 THE pretty parrot stays in the grove
Hoping for a bride
The pretty parrot stays in the grove.

In this poem, as in marriage poems, the parrot is at once a parrot and also a counter to signify a boy. Similarly, the bride is at once a girl and also a bird.

49 BROTHER, brother, your bangles
Have fallen in the water, are in the water
In the morning, your bangles
Have fallen in the water, are in the water.

[1] Dalton, *Descriptive Ethnology of Bengal*, pp. 254–255.

50 WHEN Durgan Sai is smoking his hookah
The spotted horse comes prancing and dancing
Smoking at midnight, Durgan Sai
Under the moon the spotted horse
Prances and dances.

51 *Maina, maina*, born in Jharia
*Hare*, girl, the spring days are gone
Combing the hair, parting the hair
Tying into a knot the hair
*Hare*, girl, the spring days are gone.

*Mainas* are birds like starlings and are notorious for fighting and for noisy chatter; but are easily tamed and quickly learn to talk. The Uraons often keep them as cage-birds, and it is this domestic association which probably explains their use in many poems as girl symbols.

*Hare* in this poem, or *Hare Haire* as in Poem 79, is a lament or a gasp of regret. It occasionally includes an element of triumphal mourning as in Poem 62 or pitying amusement (Poem 75).

52 IN the fishing trap he found a diamond
The diamond, will it stay with you?
Selling the diamond, will you buy a woman?
Will the woman keep?
Will the diamond last for you?

53 I PUT on my tattered clothes
And went to catch fish
On my right hip I tied a small basket
And went to catch fish.

Compare the English nursery rhyme:

"I had a little nag
That trotted up and down
I bridled him and saddled him
And trotted out of town."

54 COME, brother
Let us go to a place you have visited
If there is no place you have visited
Let us go to the land of your girl.

55 MOVING from *thana* to *thana*, brother
Do not go to Sissai *thana*
Do not go to Sissai *thana*
In Sissai *thana* the girls are sent away
Do not go to Sissai *thana*.

In this poem the reference is to the early period of recruitment for the tea gardens. The Uraons believe that during this period girls were captured, and for every girl seized a boy was caught to go with her as her "paper" husband.

A *thana* is the area under a police station. An average *thana* is twenty to thirty miles long and ten to fifteen miles wide.

56 *Sarhul* I could not dance
My *juri* has gone as a coollie
Only with him can I dance
My *juri* has gone as a coollie.

*Juri* is here translated as masculine, but it could also be feminine, and the "I" of the poem might also be either a boy or a girl. Uraon women and girls do not do ploughing, but they do almost every other form of heavy work such as transplanting paddy, reaping, carrying earth for roadwork, bringing wood from the jungle, picking tea-leaves. Female coolies are as common as male.

57 Come closer, girl, in your dress with the
coloured border
Without you there is no pleasure
Come closer, girl, come closer
The shining girl is coming.

58 Aunt, you sit by the liquor pot
As keenly as a *piyo* bird
Only for a leaf-cup of liquor
You sit by the pot like a *piyo* bird.

59 Do not ask an aunt, boy
Whether she wants to stay or go
Whether to stay or go
Did not enter the head of your uncle.

60 Old man, always you are eating figs
But there are insects in them
Morning and evening you are eating figs
But the insects are in them.

61 Old woman, you did not tell him
That there were insects in the figs
That there were insects in them
Insects insects.

## JHUMAIR

62 WHO is the girl whose time is over?
*Haire hai*
In the Ganges her ear-rings are floating
*Haire hai*
It is the flirting girl whose time is over
*Haire hai*
In the Ganges her ear-rings are floating
*Haire hai*
Who is the boy whose time is over?
*Haire hai*
Whose sash of bells is floating in the Ganges.

## CHIRDI

I HAVE not seen the Chirdi dance, but Roy describes it as a form of *Jatra* dance differing from the main *Jatra* (or *Khariah*) dances only in the tune of the songs. It is danced in *asin* and *kartik* (September to November).

63 THE mango tree is withered by the frost
The feathers of the parrot fall
Go and pick them, brother
Make a plume for the girl.

64 Go and husk the paddy, girl
The spice-coloured sun is rising
In the morning husk the paddy, girl
The spice-coloured sun is rising.

65 THE life-and-death tree blossom
Slowly swinging
In the morning and the sun
Slowly swinging.

## MATHA

66 UNDER the *peepal* tree the black cows are sitting
A heron sits on the *peepal* tree
Who was the girl who broke a branch
And sent the sitting heron flying from the tree?

67 IMAGE image image, *babu*
Image of a face with hair
When was the carving of the eight parts?
Of the father its creation
Of the mother was its birth
Out of the future were the eight parts.

*Babu*—a Hindi term of respect.

"The carving of the eight parts"—the development of the body after its conception by the parents.

# DIALOGUES FOR URAON MARRIAGES

THE use of symbolic dialogues at the stage of negotiation is fairly common among the tribes of Central India. Among the Turis, a Hinduized offshoot of the Mundas, the bridegroom's ambassador announces his business with the phrase: "I hear that a sweet-scented flower has blossomed in your house and I have come to gather it." To which the bride's father, if the match be acceptable, replies, "You may take away my flower if you will not throw it away when its sweet scent has gone."[1] Among the Khonds "a proposal for marriage is made by placing a brass cup and three arrows at the door of the girl's father. He will remove these once to show his reluctance, and they will again be replaced. If he removes them a second time, it signifies his definite refusal of the match, but if he allows them to remain, the bridegroom's friends go to him and say, "We have noticed a beautiful flower in passing through your village and desire to pluck it."[2]

An analogous method is used by the Gadarias, the occupational shepherd caste of Northern India, one of the ambassadors opening the conversation by saying, "We have the milk and you have the milk-pail; let them be joined." To which the girl's party, if the match be agreeable, will reply, "Yes, we have the tamarind and you have the mango; if the *panches* (village counsellors), agree, let there be a marriage."[3]

Roy records a similar use by Birhors when a party from the girl's house come to take the girl back to her parents a few days after the marriage. After they have settled themselves "they are asked by some elder of the bridegroom's *tanda*: 'Where do you come from? Where are you going?' They reply: 'We are come to these parts to look for strayed cattle. A herd of cattle had gone to our parts from this side. We had a she-calf. She joined the herd and came away in this direction.'

[1] R. V. Russell, *Tribes and Castes of the Central Provinces*, vol. iv, p. 590.

[2] ibid., vol. iii, pp. 467–468.

[3] Ibid., p. 5.

The first speaker replies: 'Look out for your calf then; find her out, see whither she may have gone.' 'Ah! here she is,' cries one of the bride's relatives. 'Well then,' is the reply, 'if she is your calf, you may take her home.' "[1]

The origin of these dialogues is partly in the wish for amusement—to cover the business with a film of fun; and partly in a sense of embarrassment—from the feeling that a girl's marriage is not a proper subject for higgling. This embarrassment is removed by the symbolism which retains the business nature of the talks but softens them by transferring the subject to an animal or a vegetable. In this way the brutality is removed while the business is preserved.

Of the symbols used in the three dialogues, marrow is a standard sexual image, its swelling growth being used to suggest both a ripeness for marriage and a pregnancy after marriage. In a similar way, in India as in Europe, a cow is a symbol for a woman. Deer becomes a feminine image by being an object of pursuit.

[1] S. C. Roy, *The Birhors*, pp. 206–207.

# DIALOGUES FOR URAON MARRIAGES

## THE MARROW DIALOGUE

*A (leader of the bride's party):* Who are these strangers who have come to the house in the dark?

*B (leader of the bridegroom's party):* We are only some poor travellers who have nowhere else to go. From a great distance we have come, and now the journey has left us too weak to go any further. In the hope of getting our strength back we are thinking of resting for a few days in this lovely Chota Nagpur, and when we are fit again we shall make a new start. At the moment we are famished with hunger. We have a little rice and water but no vegetables with which to make curry. Everywhere we have been looking for vegetables but getting none. Now we have heard that in this house there are some marrows, and we have come to ask if you could spare us one.

*A:* What nonsense is this? Marrows in our house? This is the house of our ancestors in which we have lived for years, and never have there been any marrows in it. We do not understand how you can have heard of any here, and in fact from what you say it looks as if you are thieves who under the pretence of asking for a marrow have come to steal our property. Get out.

*B:* No, brother, we are not thieves. You ought not to speak so sharply to hungry or thirsty strangers. Very humbly we ask you to give us what we want. We are sure some marrows are here, as we saw them on the roof. There is a particular one on which we have got our eyes, and we are set on getting it.

*A:* I am very sorry, but you are quite mistaken. There are no marrows here. But we have got a little curry, and this we will gladly give you.

*B:* I am afraid a curry will not do. It is the marrow we want.

*A:* You seem unusually set on it. It is true that before the rains we sowed a few marrow seeds. The plants have now grown up and are bearing marrows—some of them full-sized, some half-sized, while others are still very small. But as they are all on the same stalk, none of them can be picked yet. Which was the marrow you wanted? Can you describe it?

*B:* The marrow we would like is on the corner of the roof and can be easily seen from outside. It appeared to us to be a quite unusually good one—very round and with not a single blemish.

*A:* I have not seen our marrows and did not know we had one like that; but it is certainly true that there are some marrows on the roof. Here is the largest which you must have got in mind, and a very tasty curry it will make.

*B:* You will excuse us, but the big one is not the one we want. It will only spoil the curry. The half-sized one is the one we are after.

*A:* I am very sorry, but we cannot possibly part with that. We are keeping it for chutney, and besides, in order to pick it, we should have to disturb the whole stalk.

*B:* The chutney does not matter, and we will pick the marrow so carefully that none of the other marrows are damaged. If you do not mind, we will go up and get it.

*A:* Since you are so keen on getting this marrow, we withdraw our objections. But we would point out that we have all along been growing it for sale. It has cost us a good deal of time, money and labour. When the plant was young, it had to be continually watered and watched. A special gardener had to be employed. Manure had to be given. We also had to take precautions against animals. Then when it grew taller a stick had to be put for training it on to the roof. Even then our troubles did not end. When the marrow itself began to form we had to keep a watch on it to prevent it from being stolen. You can imagine the bother to which we were

# THE DEER DIALOGUE

*A (leader of the bride's party):* Who are you and what are you doing here?

*B (leader of the bridegroom's party):* We are hunters and for many years have hunted in the deep jungles of Chota Nagpur. But until now we have never had any luck. Today we had all the trouble of the chase, but at the end of it we only wounded a spotted deer and it got away. We followed the trail of its blood, and the marks led us to this door. There can't be any doubt that the deer has run to cover here. Where is it?

*A:* No wounded deer came this way. We do not keep deer in our house.

*B:* But look at the blood on the door where the deer went in. Make it over to us.

*A:* You are speaking of a deer you wounded in the jungle. There isn't any wounded deer here; but it's true there is a pet deer of ours which we have had since it was a fawn.

*B:* The only deer we want is the one we shot. Are you sure that your pet deer hasn't strayed into the jungle and got shot?

*A:* We are always extremely careful to see that it grazes near the house. You must have shot some other deer and come here by mistake.

*B:* But with our own eyes we saw the deer actually run into the house. Possibly your own deer was grazing in the jungle and got shot by accident. But as it has taken one of our arrows, we cannot give it up.

*A:* You seem very sure of this deer. Can you describe it in any detail?

*B:* We didn't get too good a view of it, as it was off as soon as we saw it. We were lucky to hit it with an arrow; and after that the trail of blood brought us here.

*A:* That doesn't get us very far. It is quite obvious that you haven't shot our pet deer; and are trying to bluff. What was the age of the deer? And what was its colour?

*B:* As I said, we didn't get a good view of the deer; but it seemed to us to be full-grown and dappled in colour.

*A:* The description tallies with our pet deer, but would you be able to pick it out if we put it with some others?

*B:* Yes. We should know it again if we saw it—that deer which has brought us so far without any food or drink.

*A:* Then there is nothing more to say. It must have been our deer which you shot while it was grazing. And since you have shot it, we shall have to make it over to you. But remember that it has lived here ever since it was born, and we have had a good deal of trouble in bringing it up. Its mother was very rich in milk, and unless you have numerous fields and a large jungle it won't be happy with you.

*B:* Don't worry about that. It will be quite all right with us. There are several jungles close by and plenty of green pastureland. It will be able to go from jungle to jungle and field to field without any danger. We don't allow any hunters in our jungles. It will even be better off than it is at present.

*A:* There is something in what you say. But after all, the place will seem strange to it, and it may not like it. Still, since it belongs to you, we have nothing to say. Before we actually give it up, though, you should pay us back all that we have spent on it.

*B:* As we shot the deer with our own arrow, it obviously belongs to us. But we do not want to be unpleasant and take it without paying you your expenses. How much did you have to spend on bringing it up?

The bride-price is then discussed and the dialogue concludes.

*Gumla thana.* 1936.

of water, and she went inside your door. In this way and without any accident we safely reached your house.

*B:* Father of the bridegroom, I am extremely pleased to hear you say it. You have come on a truly auspicious day. Good luck to you.

Gumla *thana*. 1936.

put and will understand that we cannot just give it away for nothing.

*B:* We quite appreciate all the time and labour which have gone to growing it, and we do not want it for nothing. We are quite willing to pay a price.

*Gumla.* 1936.

## THE COW DIALOGUE

*A (leader of the bridegroom's party):* Friends, we heard that one of our lost cows has come to your village and is in your cowshed.

*B (leader of the bride's party):* Yes. There is a cow which has been in our cowshed for a long time. Perhaps you would know it if you saw it? Is it white, black, red or grey? Here are the cows.

*A:* Friends, we are in luck's way. That grey cow over there is the very cow which has been missing for a long time. Now we have found it. I am afraid we shan't be able to pay you anything for keeping it so long, but we will just take it away.

*B:* As it is your property, of course, we do not claim it. But we would like to know what happened while you were looking for it. And as it has been in our cowshed for so long, we shall naturally feel sorry at parting with it so quickly. But it obviously belongs to you, so what can we say?

*A:* You quite properly ask for certain information. And I shall try to give it. While the sun was rising in the east, the parrots were screaming together and were eating the ants in the *cheetka* tree. Twelve girls with newly washed hands and feet were coming from the spring in new clothes carrying fresh water on their heads. We stopped and had some banter with them. After that we met a royal youth who was bringing from a great distance his horse, elephant, *doli* and *palki*. Owing to this, the road was full of dust and the drums were rolling like thunder. We were able, however, to reach your house in safety—the thorns not pricking us and no lizard crossing the path, and no jackal howled. Just before we reached your house we saw a girl with a pot

# OMENS

LIKE a belief in the influence of the stars, a belief in omens springs from a sense of the connectedness of phenomena. But unlike the stars, an omen itself does not influence a line of action. It merely indicates that a certain train of events is in operation and suggests the consequences if a certain line of action is pursued. Just as a piece of litmus paper tests whether a solution is acid or alkali, an omen tests the sum of circumstances at a particular time.

Omens are almost always general symbols of "life" and "death", "prosperity" and "failure"—terms to which all projects can ultimately be reduced. Consequently when a particular project is in hand, such as a marriage, a party has no difficulty in using the traditional symbol as a symbol of its particular case. And since the symbol is for the time being the object which it symbolizes, the appearance of the omen is easily taken to involve the future occurrence of the event. An omen is in fact a symbol of the future seen in the present, and for this reason it is able to act as a test.

Among the Uraons all omens are capable of this analysis.

## BAD OMENS

(1) A thorn pricking. This is a bad omen because it implies a wound which may mean a loss of blood and a corresponding loss of vitality; or alternatively because it implies a sore which will act as a check.

(2) A lizard. As a cold-blooded creature this is an "anti-life" symbol.

(3) An empty pitcher. This indicates an absence of water which from its life-giving powers is a normal "vitality" symbol.

(4) An empty-handed girl. The absence of property or wealth. Equals poverty.

(5) A woman carrying ashes or clothes in an earthen vessel. These are carried for washing purposes and symbolize weakness, as new clothes would symbolize strength.

(6) A dead animal being removed. The destruction of property.

(7) A snake in the path. A danger symbol.

(8) A vulture overhead. As a vulture feeds on carrion it tends to be associated with death. The fact that the vulture is overhead shows that it is waiting and that a death is imminent. The imminence rather than the actual occurrence of a death is bad; since once a death has occurred, death is temporarily out of the way.

(9) Hearing an owl. The owl's cry as in England suggests harm and horror.

(10) Hearing a jackal. As a jackal feeds on carrion, its cry has the same meaning as the waiting vulture. The howl indicates the temporary absence of death but its future possibility.

—

# OMENS

The annual fairs and *jatras* also provide opportunities for "inspection". But these can scarcely be said to provide conditions for *courtship*, and it is only in the village or its immediate neighbourhood that an Uraon boy has the opportunity of seeing very much of a particular girl. Such a friendship very rarely ends in marriage, as the tribal rule is for a boy to be married *outside* his neighbourhood. It is noteworthy that although I made particular inquiries on this point in Manda and Jashpur *thanas*, none of the old men whom I questioned either knew of any instance of marriage by choice or had heard of it as a previous custom. It therefore seems unlikely that "a perfect understanding" between the boy and girl can ever have been general; and it is likely that the form of selection by the parents has always been a reality. Possibly, however, if the marriage age was later than it is at present, an element of suggestion from the boy and girl may have influenced the parents in making the negotiations. But such a suggestion would have been based more on a casual sight than on an actual friendship. Nowadays, with the fall in the marriage age, even this element is wanting.

*Negotiation preliminaries.*—On being authorized to proceed, the chief negotiator in Gumla *thana* approaches the girl's family and makes the proposal. The girl's parents usually take ten days to consult their relatives and inquire about the boy, and then on their side they select a man as negotiator to convey their decision. This man meets the agent of the boy, and if the girl's family is found to approve of the marriage he informs the agent of their willingness. A date about ten days later is then fixed for a clinching ceremony at the girl's house.

*The journey to the clinching ceremony.*—For this step a party consisting of the boy, the boy's parents, relatives and neighbours comprising an odd number such as seven, eleven or thirteen visits the girl's parents. The journey is undertaken in the light of omens,[1] and if any bad omens are encountered, the more orthodox Uraons will abandon the marriage. The less strict Uraons, however, regard omens as a form of play

[1] See p. 159 below.

and take them less seriously. Examples of bad omens are a lizard crossing the path, a pitcher lying empty, an empty-handed girl entering a house, and a thorn pricking. Good omens are the sight on starting or arrival of a lamp burning, a corpse being carried, or a pitcher filled with water.

*The journey dialogue: the clinching ceremony.*—On arrival at the girl's house the boy's party is admitted and a formal dialogue ensues—the girl's parents feigning ignorance of the purpose of the visit and questioning the party about its object. This object is never stated as an inquiry about the girl, but is always translated into an image-system in which a vegetable, a deer or a cow are used as counters. The party is then interrogated about its journey and the kind of omens it encountered, and if these are satisfactory a conversation is then introduced regarding the price to be paid for the girl. Most villages have certain customary rates such as seven pieces of cloth and five rupees, and when the usual rate is proposed it is at once accepted. The girl's parents then ask the boy if he is willing to marry the girl, and on the boy confirming this the girl is told to come with a *lota* or pot of water. When this is brought, first the boy and then the girl drink from it; and after this it is passed round and each of the parties takes a sip.[1] The giving and acceptance of the water clinches the contract, and after a date for a return visit has been fixed the girl's parents give the boy's party some food, and with the singing of marriage poems the meeting then breaks up.

In certain other parts of Gumla *thana* the procedure is the same, but with the important difference that when the party leaves for the girl's house the boy is left behind and the sacrament of water is done with his parents and agent. On these occasions after the bride-price has been settled, the girl is brought in with a *lota* of water on her head and is put on the knees of the boy's leader. Some water is then poured into a cup, and first the girl drinks and then the leader, and after

[1] Grignard notes the variation that the girl gives the *lota* to the boy, and that the boy then places it on her head and takes it down. The total action signifies the agreement. Hahn's *Oraon Folk-lore*, p. 10.

this the two parties drink from the same water. The girl remains on the leader's knees while the water is circulating, and when this is finished she is put down and is admonished to respect the cats and dogs of her parents' home and those of her prospective husband. She is also warned that though the iron tie may break, the tie of the skin will never break. After this the dates are settled, the boy's party is fed, and the meeting breaks up.

*Variation of the procedure* (a) *Jashpur thana.*—In Jashpur *thana* the procedure is slightly different. In this area separate visits are made for each of the stages—a party consisting of the boy's father and two others visiting the girl's house to settle the bride-price and a similar party from the girl's side visiting the boy's house to settle the date for the clinching ceremony. At both visits the symbolic dialogue occurs and both visits are scrutinized in the light of omens. On the occasion of the visit by the girl's party the boy's father is questioned whether any horse, buffalo or cow has died in the village, and only if there has been no death does the party enter. After this visit omens do not operate.

Unlike the practice in Gumla *thana*, the clinching ceremony in Jashpur always takes place in the boy's house, and only very rarely, when the girl's family is unusually prosperous, is it also done as an additional ceremony in the house of the girl. The ceremony in Jashpur *thana* is known as *gharbari pahi*, or the inspection of the house. About thirty of the girl's friends and relatives arrive at the boy's house, and after their feet have been washed and rice-beer has been served three *lotas* are produced. Each *lota* is filled not with water but with rice-beer. The girl's father then presents one of the *lotas* to the boy's father; a man from the girl's side gives a *lota* to a man from the boy's side, and the third *lota* is given by a woman of the girl's side to a woman of the boy's side. The persons receiving the *lotas* pour a little of the rice-beer into leaf-cups, and then pour out a little for the persons who gave the *lotas*. After these have drunk the *lotas* are circulated among the parties, and everyone drinks a little from them. The date of the wedding is then fixed. Neither the girl nor the boy attend the ceremony.

*Variation of the procedure* (b) *Mahuadanr thana.*—In Mahuadanr there is yet another variation. As in Gumla *thana*, the discussion of the bride-price is part of the clinching ceremony, but the *gharbari pahi*, or house-inspection, is separate and does not occur until immediately prior to the marriage a year or two later.

The essence of the clinching ceremony in this area consists in the presentation of some grain by the boy's father to the girl's parents and the anointing of his feet by the girl's mother. There is then some feasting, during which the girl comes in with a pot of rice-beer on her head and stands before the boy's father. The boy's father takes the pot from her head, embraces her, and gives her a rupee. For the remainder of the feast the girl sits at his feet.

The "house-inspection" ceremony occurs in the boy's house and consists of a reunion of the parents. The villagers "all gather before the house where a bower has been erected; both fathers sit together on a special mat in the middle. At a given signal they both get up, and when silence is gained they join arms and one of them says: "Above God, below the *panch.*[1] He who wishes to cut, let him cut now. What is joined with iron can be separated, what is joined with skin cannot be separated." The other one in his turn repeats the same sentence and adds: "Now is the time to say the right word." All the party then puts an end to this imposing scene by shouting in chorus, "*Hogaya, hogaya*—it is done." Two boys then step in and anoint both fathers with oil. Then they eat and drink and make merry till the evening of the following day.[2]

*Summary.*—Prior to the actual wedding then the procedure may be outlined as involving

(1) The provisional selection of a girl by the boy's parents;
(2) informal negotiations leading to a provisional acceptance

[1] The agent.
[2] P. Dehon, *The Religion and Customs of the Uraons*, p. 162.

(3) a formal visit which is tested by omens;
(4) the settlement of a bride-price;
(5) a clinching ceremony; and
(6) a ceremony of "house-inspection" involving a union of the fathers.

The variations of procedure in the three areas may be summarized by saying that in Gumla *thana* the discussion of the bride-price is part of the clinching ceremony and there is no ceremony of "house-inspection". In Jashpur *thana* the discussion of the bride-price is separate from the clinching ceremony, but the latter is part of the ceremony of "house-inspection". In Mahuadanr *thana* the discussion of the bride-price is part of the clinching ceremony, but the house-inspection ceremony is separate and does not occur until later.

## *B.* THE MARRIAGE

### (I) GUMLA *THANA*

*The arrival of the bridegroom's party.*—The wedding day then comes. Paddy sheaves are tied round some earthen pitchers, and carrying the pitchers on their heads and the bride-price in a basket and taking some water and rice-beer with them the bridegroom's party set out for the bride's village. The bridegroom carries a sword, and if the family is well-to-do he travels in a *palki* or rides on a pony. The party arrange to arrive after dark, and on arrival to halt under some trees outside the village while the chief agent goes on to tell the bride's party of their arrival. Some water and rice-beer are then drunk while the bride-price is being verified and the bridegroom's party is being counted to ascertain how many have come. If the number is found to be large, the bride's parents say, "We have invited you to sit, but we cannot make you stand." The bridegroom's party then make their own arrangements for food.

*The fusion of the parties.*—About midnight the girl's party emerge from the village—married women who have had children going first, some paddy-draped pitchers on their heads, while the old women come after, bearing *lotas* of water with mango leaves. Candles are lit on the pitchers and the drums start to beat. As the procession slowly moves out the men and women dance and marriage poems are sung, while simultaneously the bridegroom's party comes into movement. The pitchers are put on the heads. Candles are lit. The parties converge. The women with the pitchers dance face to face. With the linking of the parties the old women come out and sprinkle water with mango twigs over the bridegroom's party.

*Wedding preliminaries.*—During the process of fusion the bridegroom is taken from his party and is carried to the bride's house by a member of the family. There he finds the door shut, and to get it opened he pays a rupee. The door is then opened and the bridegroom goes inside. Here his hands and feet are washed and he is placed on a mat. While this is being done the pitchers of the bridegroom's party are brought into the room and the rest of the party are allowed to troop in until the burning of some chillies indicates that the men must go. They then go into the courtyard and sit under the *marwa* or marriage bower. This consists of three lines in each of which there are three *sal* poles with a roofing of foliage. The bride and bridegroom are then smeared with *haldi* (spice) and their foreheads are rubbed with oil. Finally, at cock-crow the women who carried the pitchers take them out into the courtyard and start to dance; and as they dance the central ceremony begins.

*The central ceremony.*—For this a mat is first turned round the bridegroom three times and is then spread on the ground. Five handfuls of thatching grass, then a yoke and then a grinding-stone are put on the mat, and over these some *sal* leaves are strewn. Five pieces of *haldi*, five nuts, five copper coins, and a little sunned rice are then put on the leaves, and over these the bride and bridegroom stand—the girl taking a position in front of the boy. They are then screened off with a piece of cloth, and an old woman gives the boy some *sindur* or scarlet powder to dab on the girl's forehead. The girl then puts some powder on the boy's forehead, and after that the boy presses the heels of the girl with his toes[1] and a *lota* of water is sprinkled on their heads. The marriage is then complete.

*The invocation of the ancestors.*—After this the party goes with the bridegroom to a field on the eastern side of the village—the boy's father, the girl's father and the *pahan* each carrying a *lota* of water. The bridegroom and through her father the

[1] Roy notes the detail that the boy presses the big toe and second toe of his left foot against the left heel of the girl and encloses it like a fork. (S. C. Roy, *Oraon Religion and Customs*, p. 157.) Among Kurmis, when the bride and bridegroom walk seven times round the marriage post the bride leads and the bridegroom comes after with his left hand on her left shoulder. (R. V. Russell, *Tribes and Castes of the Central Provinces*, vol. iv, pp. 61–66.) This emphasis on the left side may be a form of symbolism based on the location of the heart.

bride are then abjured to respect each other's ancestors and the *lotas* of water are held up in formal emphasis. The party then returns to the marriage bower. On their arrival the bride-price is formally brought out and made over to the party of the bride, and the bride and bridegroom are taken inside.

*The giving of presents.*—The scene then becomes festive. Rice-beer is served, riddles are put, and the morning passes in drinking and the singing of marriage poems. After that the morning meal is taken and the parties relax until the mid-afternoon, when everyone again assembles for the ceremony of *chumawan* or present-giving.

For this ceremony the bride and bridegroom emerge in new clothes and sit under the marriage bower but not on the yoke or grinding-stone. A cloth is then put over them and the three metal dishes containing spice, spice-coloured rice and some cut-up nuts, coconut and dates are placed in front of them. A man sits beside them with a drum, and as he beats it he calls on the guests to let the clouds rain. On this the women come in one by one, each woman sprinkling a little of the coloured rice on the couple, dabbing some spice on their foreheads and putting an anna in the dish with the rice. The couple gives each woman in return a pinch of nuts. As each woman finishes another woman is drummed in by the man with the drum.

*The marriage sermon.*—When the present-giving is over a marriage sermon is delivered by one of the older men and women; and at its conclusion the bride and bridegroom are led inside the house.

*The farewell address, the departure for the bridegroom's house.*—With this the marriage moves to its close. Another meal is served to the parties, the presents are collected, the bride and bridegroom change their clothes and the parties then form up for a return to the bridegroom's village. The bridegroom's party is seen off to the outskirts of the bride's village, and near the village boundary the bride's brother formally makes her over to her husband. A short farewell address is given to her by her father and she is also presented with an arrow.

The bridegroom's party then lifts her up and starts on the march home.

*The entry into the bridegroom's family.*—On arriving at her husband's house the girl finds the door shut and has to pay a few annas for admission. She is then taken inside, is washed and anointed; and after that she is considered to be a member of her husband's family.

*The return visits.*—About a fortnight after the marriage a party from the girl's house pays a return visit. The bridegroom's party meet it at the outskirts of the village, escort it to a bower in the boy's house and supply the guests with rice-beer. Some hours are then passed in drinking and in the singing of marriage poems; and after a feast the party breaks up and the members return home. A fortnight later the boy and girl go to the girl's house and stay with her parents for a week; and on their return they start living in a separate house of their own.[1]

## (2) JASHPUR *THANA*

The procedure in this *thana* follows the main structure of the practice in Gumla but at the same time differs in many items. The central ceremony, for instance, is on the whole similar, but it takes place not at the girl's house but at the boy's. It is not preceded by any greeting dance and is not followed by a farewell address. There is also a different invocation of the ancestors. At the same time there are items in Jashpur which do not occur in Gumla. In Jashpur there are two arrivals and not one—the men and women coming in separate parties. A best man and a bride's maid are used, and the guests are elaborately annointed. There is also a declaration of family union, a ceremonial eating of a rice cake, and a formal drawing of water.

As there seems no obvious way of combining the two accounts, I am appending a separate description.

[1] If the boy and girl are young, this process of living together is postponed, the girl remaining with her parents.

*The arrival of the girl's party (men).*—At about midday on the day prior to the wedding an advance party from the girl's side arrives, and these go out and meet the main body of men which arrives in the evening. As the guests come in the women of the boy's family rub their legs with oil and wash their feet, and they receive an anna from each guest in return. The girl's party then squats in the courtyard beneath the marriage bower and is given rice-beer, a pig and a castrated goat. Their legs are again rubbed with oil by the village youths, and after this the girl's father and two other men from the girl's side and the boy's father with two other men from the boy's side form up for a marriage declaration.

*The marriage declaration.*—For the purpose of this declaration the men from the girl's side stand in a line facing the east, while the men from the boy's side stand in a line facing them. Each man puts his arms on the shoulders of the man opposite. A declaration is then made that each side is now related to the other, that five handfuls of grass from the girl's village can be used for thatching the boy's house, and three handfuls of grass from the boy's village can be used for thatching the girl's house, and that if a dog of either house comes it will be welcomed in both houses.

*The picking up of the bridegroom.*—Some time after this declaration, which occurs at about midnight, the bridegroom appears carrying two pots of rice-beer on a stick and accompanied by two companions. The leaders of the girl's party receive the pots, and the bridegroom is then picked up, carried into the middle of the *marwa* and placed on the knees of one of the girl's leaders. The leader who takes him salutes the company present.

*The arrival of the girl with the girl's party (women).*—This takes place at about 3 a.m., and by this time the men of the girl's party have eaten, and with the exception of the girl's father and the leaders they then depart. At about the same time the girl and the women of her party reach the village. Usually the girl arrives on foot, but if her parents are well-to-do she is brought on a chair or *palki*.

*The massage of the bride and bridegroom.*—On their arrival the women are given two guards and are washed, massaged and fed by the women of the boy's family. The boy and girl are then brought out at cock-crow and made to stand on a mat while their bodies are massaged by women of the opposite party.

*The eating of the rice cake and the formal drawing of water.*—A cake of rice is then wrapped in a new cloth and put on top of a new earthen pot. The bride's sister takes it, and leaving the bride behind goes down with the other women to a spring where all of them wash and the cake is eaten. The pot is then filled with water, and the bride's sister brings it back to the house. The central ceremony follows.

*The central ceremony.*—For this a grinding stone is covered with straw and placed near the *marwa*, and over it a yoke is put. The boy then comes with a companion, who acts as his "best man", and takes up his position on the yoke. The girl is then led in by a "bride's maid" and takes her stand immediately behind the boy. The boy puts one of his feet on the girl's ankles. The boy's mother then presents a vermilion box to the "best man", who takes the boy's right hand, dips the index finger in the powder and makes a scarlet mark with it on the girl's forehead. The bride's maid then makes a similar mark on the boy's forehead with the girl's finger—the box being produced by the girl's mother. The boy and girl are then screened off by means of a long piece of cloth, while the bride's sister takes some water from the pot and sprinkles it first on the couple and then on the guests. The sprinkling ends with a shout, and on this the boy and girl with their two companions hurry into the house. From there they go into the *bari* or garden plot attached to the house and are washed by their companions. They come out clad in new clothes given by the boy's father and go back into the house with their companions. There they wait while the *dhela* ceremony or invocation of the ancestors is performed.

*The invocation of the ancestors.*—For this five *sal* leaves are placed end to end on the eastern side of the *bari*, and on two of the leaves two small pots are placed. At the same time two pots of rice-beer are put by the *marwa*. The husband of the girl's sister and the husband of the boy's sister then take up the pots of rice-beer and fill the small pots which are on the leaves. The two fathers then take up the small pots and offer them to the ancestors, abjuring the boy and girl to call upon them in time of trouble and stating that from now on the ancestors of both the families will be available to both. The party then goes back to the *marwa*, and all the men then have their morning meal.

*The giving of presents.*—After this the *chumawan* or present-giving is done. The boy and girl sit in the *marwa* with the "best man" and "bride's maid" on either side and the two grandmothers standing behind. The men of the two parties squat on one side and the women on the other. Two plates of rice and one of tamarind are then put in front of the boy and girl; and the women come up in turn, sprinkle rice on them and deposit small money presents in the dishes.

*The marriage sermon.*—Later in the afternoon there is a return to the grinding-stone, the straw and the yoke. The boy and girl are brought in and are put on the yoke. The girl's brother-in-law then preaches her a short marriage sermon warning her to look carefully at the boy and not complain afterwards that she did not see him or that he is lame or blind, and telling her that she must always look after him and care for him. He then gives her a leaf-cup of rice-beer. A similar sermon is given to the boy by his brother-in-law. Some water is then sprinkled on the boy and girl, the tension is relaxed and the wedding party then breaks up into groups of chatting men and women.

*The entry into the boy's family.*—Early in the evening another meal is served, and the girl's father then tells the boy's father that he is formally making over his daughter to him. The women then return home, and the girl's brother picks her up and carries her to the door of the boy. There the girl pays an anna to the boy's younger brother or sister, and on this the door is opened and the girl goes in. Those who have not eaten then take their meals. The "best man" tells the girl to spread a mat, and she and the boy lie down together. The following day the *marwa* is pulled down and the remaining relatives go home.

*Return visits.*—As the girl's family is not expected to be able to afford the cost of entertainment, there is no return visit of the boy's party, but a fortnight after the marriage the boy and the girl go and stay a few days with the girl's parents.

### (3) MAHUADANR *THANA*[1]

In this *thana*, as at Jashpur, the central ceremony takes place at the boy's house, but the arrival of the girl is preceded by a mimic fight[2] which blends into a greeting dance. Unlike Gumla, the paddy-draped pitchers are not brought out for the dance; but after the girl's party has arrived, and the evening meal has been eaten, there is a separate blessing dance by two of the women.

*The blessing dance.*—For this dance some rice, turmeric and oil-seed are put in a small pitcher. Some paddy stalks are then put on top—the ears being divided into two parts by bringing some of the stems over the ears. A small lamp is lit in the hollow formed by the ears. A big rice cake is then placed in a basket, and two women with scarlet on their foreheads then dance before the bride and bridegroom—one taking the pitcher and the other taking the basket on her head. As they dance they sing marriage songs.

*The central ceremony* follows the practice at Gumla.

*The invocation of the ancestors.*—This does not occur outside the village as in Gumla or in the boy's garden as at Jashpur, but takes place in the marriage bower. Six leaf-cups with two small earthen pots are put on a mat, and the two fathers squat before them. Each then takes up a pitcher of rice-beer which has been dedicated with scarlet and pours some beer into three of the cups. As they pour they reach across each other's arms

1 P. Dehon, *The Religion and Customs of the Uraons*, pp. 161–164.

2 Compare Poems 133–135 below.

and seek the blessing of the ancestors on the marriage. Some beer is then spilt on the ground as an offering and leaf-cups of rice-beer are distributed among the guests.

*The salute of the guests.*—In Mahuadanr this takes the place of the giving of presents, and consists of the boy and girl being reanointed with oil and scarlet, tied together by a knot made with their clothes, and then being sent round the company to pay their respects. This leads on to another ceremony which also does not occur in Gumla or Jashpur.

*The pledge of the bridegroom's brother.*—For this the bride brings a cup of rice-beer in the privacy of the two families, and instead of putting it in the hand of the bridegroom's brother she deposits it on the ground in front of him. "This is to seal a tacit agreement that from that time the brother of the bridegroom will never touch the wife of his brother."

*The marriage sermon* follows the same lines as at Gumla.

*The entry into the boy's family.*—Here it is the mother who makes the girl over to the boy, telling him as she does so that the girl is being given for good and that he must love and look after her. The boy's companion then seizes her in his arms and carries the girl into the boy's house.

## C. SYMBOLISM

It will be obvious that many objects used in the ceremonies are symbols and that the ceremonies themselves have a symbolic character.

The main idea of marriage is the union of the boy and the girl and of the two families. This is symbolized either by a physical contact, an exchange or by a sharing in a common act. Thus at the clinching ceremony the boy and girl drink from the same pot. The water or rice-beer is shared by the whole company. The girl is embraced by the boy's leader and is placed on his knees. At the arrival for the marriage the idea of union is expressed in the sprinkling of the whole party with mango leaves, and at the actual wedding by the embrace of the boy by the girl's leader. The boy and girl also stand at the same spot. They exchange the scarlet powder. The boy presses the girl's heels. Water is sprinkled on both their heads. Presents are exchanged with the guests, and in Jashpur a rice cake is jointly eaten by the women of the two families. Dehon notes that the plaited stems on the paddy-draped pitchers are also intended to symbolize union.

The significance of the ritual lies not only in the simple symbolism of the action but also in the basic quality of the symbols through which the action works. The objects used are either "life", "fertility" or economic symbols. Water and the evergreen mango are "life" symbols. The scarlet powder is a blood substitute. Rice, nuts and dates are symbols of fertility; while at the central ceremony the thatching grass, yoke and grinding-stone are economic symbols, stressing the fact that a marriage means a home. The procedure is, as it were, a diagram of all that is most fundamental in life.

# MARRIAGE POEMS

## I

THERE are no Uraon love poems: there are only marriage poems. This is not because Uraons do not love but because the concern of the poems is with the publicly sanctioned and the publicly observed. Love is not the basis on which Uraons marry, but marriage is the only sexual relation which Uraons recognize. Consequently, even if love develops within their marriages it is not felt to be urgent and is not regarded as necessary. As in the West, marital love tends to be taken for granted and the institution disguises the feelings. A marriage poem is never a love poem.

Similarly, although there is flirtation before marriage, love affairs are not recognized, and although a few poems deal with the spectacle of the flirting boy, it is always from the outside and never from the heart. There is no Uraon equivalent of

> O western wind when wilt thou blow
>   That the small rain down can rain
> Christ that my love were in my arms
>   And I in my bed again.

In Uraon poems passion is neither observed nor approved.

To the tribe as a whole marriage is a duty, a necessity, and on the whole a happiness. A family is proud to receive a daughter-in-law and the girl's parents are proud to obtain the marriage status for her.

> "You have married your daughter
> You have done well
> Your house is empty
> You have got a daughter-in-law
> You have done well
> Your house is brightened."

"Say goodbye, mother
You will stay in the house
You have lost your daughter and found a son."

As in England, there is a note of congratulation at a wedding —a sense that the act has public approval. For their part, a boy and a girl would much sooner be married than not married; and in the long run they expect to be happy.

Beneath the sense of approval, however, is a sense of grief— the desolation of the family at losing a daughter, the girl's anguish at leaving her home. In the negotiation period and again when the period of adjustment after marriage is over the former feeling predominates. But the second level of feeling is probably acutest at the wedding when the disintegration of the family is imminent. The Uraon attitude to marriage is consequently not so much a fixed feeling as a succession or conflict of feelings which oscillate round the wedding.

In the marriage poems it is the feeling of grief which predominates. This is because the poems are mainly sung at the wedding itself and consequently take their tone from the prevailing attitude. And this attitude, while seeing in the wedding a cause of congratulation, deems it more correct to emphasize the girl's grief. As a result the poems are rather exaggerations of a single element in the Uraon attitude than expressions of a complete or considered view. The element of grief acts as a distorting agent which minimizes the gayer aspects.

Examples of this action are the terms in which the parents-in-law are referred to. A degree of hostility is latent in all relationships of daughter-in-law and parents-in-law; but in Uraon families this is offset by a genuine delight at receiving a new daughter. In the poems, however, the parents-in-law are always referred to as if they were the girl's enemies. Even her own parents are sometimes treated as her enemies because they have delivered her to her parents-in-law.

"Go east go west
But never to a father-in-law."

The opposite aspect of this grief distortion is the exaggerated feeling for the home and the girl's place in it. In most Uraon households there is a good deal of family affection, but the parents are not stunned when a girl has to leave home on marriage. Similarly the status of wife draws a girl to her husband. But in the poems the girl is the life of her parents and her departure is death.

## 2

Marriage poems fall into two groups. The first consists of "documentary" poems—poems which describe the dress of the bridegroom or the details of a procession and consist of literal statements of marriage facts.

"The scabbard and sword are going
The drums are beating
The red chair is carried
The dancers come."

The second consists of poems which use the twin levels of an image system—the poems being apparently about objects of nature but actually referring to aspects of marriage.

The way this system works is shown in a small group of "clue" poems.

"The fawns frolic in the ploughed fields
No. It is not the *sambar*. It is not the barking deer.
This is the girl selected by the father
The bride chosen by the mother."

The importance of these "clue" poems is that they dissect the image and expose a level of submerged meaning, thus indicating that the poem is meant to work through the interaction of the two levels. In the majority of the marriage poems the subsidiary level remains submerged, the marriage context being all that indicates its presence.

"Under, under the hills
The spring has broken
There, mother, the cobras are moving
Mother, the cobras are moving."

The "clue" poems are consequently of the greatest importance, for they keep the other poems active and ensure that the tribe will always be alive to the method.[1]

In certain poems a slight distortion is used to expose the second meaning. In Poem 92, for example, the fig-tree blossom becomes the girl because the scent spreads for forty miles. The news of the girl's eligibility could spread for this distance, but the scent could not. In Poem 91 the calf becomes the girl because it belongs to the mother. In this way part of the object symbolized is added to the image symbolizing it and the system appears through the distortion.

A similar use occurs in Poem 93, where the second level is exposed by changing the sex of an image.

"Every house has red *brinjals*
My own house has a small *brinjal*
Buy it, daughter of a vegetable seller
Hearing it the tears fall."

[1] Compare André Breton, *What is Surrealism?* p. 34: "If one thinks of the extraordinary hold that Lautréamont's celebrated phrase, 'Beautiful as the chance meeting of a sewing-machine and an umbrella on a dissecting-table,' can take upon the mind, and if one cares to make use of the key of the simplest sexual images, it should not take one long to realize that this hold owes its strength to the fact that the umbrella represents the man, the sewing-machine the woman, and the dissecting-table the bed."

Compare also T. S. Eliot, *Ash Wednesday*, II:

"Lady, three white leopards sat under a juniper tree
In the cool of the day, having fed to satiety
On my legs my heart my liver and that which had been contained
In the hollow round of my skull"

where the three white leopards are not simply leopards but are also the destructive impulses of the heart. This simultaneous suspension of two meanings through an image system is the method of Uraon marriage poems.

In this poem the boy's agent is a male and should therefore have been the vegetable seller himself. The vegetable seller becomes his daughter in order that her sex may be transferred to the *brinjals* and make it plain that they are girls. The presence of the tears is a further distortion which shows that the *brinjals* are not as simple as they seem.

In many poems, however, there is no distortion and the second level is detected by the marriage context in which the poems are used and by the employment of pantomimic images. In Poems 105 and 106, for instance, the wild buffaloes and the cobras are equated with opposing relatives because their actions are similar. The action of a bridegroom's party in descending on the girl's house is paralleled in a line of storks descending on a river or a flock of sparrows settling on a tree. A leaping member of the bridegroom's party acts like a frog. The actions of negotiators in closing round a girl resemble bees round a flower and spiders on a web. In these poems the marriage context suffices to show that the images are pantomimic and the accuracy of the pantomime exposes the symbol.

In the poems which relate to the bride and the bridegroom the clue remains in the context, but the types of symbol vary more widely. Those of the bridegroom consist either of colour analogies ("the green parrot") or power images (the bear, the tiger, the otter). In the case of the bride, certain images are based on the comparison of qualities. Doves, pigeons, wild geese and fish, for instance, possess varying qualities of elegance and speed which resemble the grace or flirtatiousness of a girl; while calves and fawns resemble a girl in their weakness and dependence. Certain other images, such as *brinjals*, mangoes, figs and bamboos are based on sexual parallels—the connection being either visual or through a fertility power.

In all the poems it is the marriage context—the presence of an audience for a marriage purpose—which enables the images to be used without explanation, and in fact to form an image-system. They do not need to refer to the objects they symbolize because the occasion itself makes the audience see them as symbols.

In England the absence of fixed occasions for poetry is perhaps a reason why English imagery has hitherto been lacking in this "public" symbolism. It is true that in the sixteenth and seventeenth centuries certain trees and plants were habitually associated with certain situations and ceremonies—the yew and cypress with death and funerals, the oak, laurel and myrtle with heroism and celebrations of victory; and in this way certain images had acquired a symbolism deriving from the conventional use of their subjects. When these images were used in poems, however, the conventional use was always introduced as part of the poem. For example

"Lay a garland on my hearse
 Of the dismal yew;
Maidens, willow branches bear;
 Say, I died true."

(*John Fletcher*)

Here the yew is introduced as part of a funeral. It does not replace the funeral, neither is the funeral left to be inferred from it. The symbol is merely an ornament. If this had been an Uraon poem, the context would have supplied the reference. The hearse would have been contained in the yew.

In a similar way certain flowers have a stock symbolism in English verse. The lily is a symbol of virginity, the rose is a symbol of passion, the honeysuckle is a symbol of attraction. These symbols, however, are normally accompanied by a note of explanation. Compare the following examples:

"Roses blushing as they blow
And enticing men to pull
Lilies whiter than the snow
Woodbines of sweet honey full
*All love's emblems*, and all cry
'Ladies, if not pluck'd, we die."

(*John Fletcher*)

"The lilies and languors *of virtue*
The roses and raptures *of vice*."
(*Swinburne*)

The reason is that without a social context the symbolism is uncertain. A poem about a rose has to show that it is a love poem, as otherwise it may only be a flower piece.

In modern English poetry there is a frequent use of symbolic images, and so far its methods and those of Uraon marriage poems tend to coincide. On the other hand, unlike Uraon poetry and most earlier poetry in England, the symbolism tends to be private and its interpretation depends not so much on a public convention as on the total "charge" of the individual poem. In the absence of a public context such as the Uraon, and in the absence of explanations as in the seventeenth century, an element of obscurity seems a necessary condition of its real gain in range and power.

# MARRIAGE POEMS

(*a*) PRE-MARRIAGE: THE *CHAILA*

(*b*) PRE-MARRIAGE: THE RIPE GIRL

(*c*) NEGOTIATION:

(1) the search for the bride
(2) the arrival of the negotiators
(3) attempt and opposition: the discussion process
(4) attempt and success
(5) attempt and failure
(6) the selected girl

(*d*) THE CLINCHING CEREMONY

(*e*) THE MARRIAGE:

(1) the appearance of the bridegroom
(2) the arrival of the bridegroom's party
(3) the mock capture
(4) the wedding presents
(5) the apparatus of marriage
(6) the emotions of the boy and the girl
(7) the departure of the bride and bridegroom

(*f*) THE RESULTS OF MARRIAGE:

(1) "the death of the heart"—the village, the family, the girl
(2) the destruction of friendships
(3) the bride in the husband's house

## (*a*) PRE-MARRIAGE: THE *CHAILA*

"THE path to the spring" figures in many Uraon poems as a place for flirtation and "girl inspection". It is the place to which all the village girls have to go every day for washing and for bringing the day's supply of water. Usually Uraon girls go there in a small band and usually at the same time every day. A boy who is "girl-mad" will therefore hang about near the path to the spring in the hopes of being able to get into conversation or of being able to impress. Similarly, when an agent from a boy's house wishes to see a girl before commencing marriage talks with her parents, he gets a villager to show the girl to him as she goes down to the spring for water. This gives him a chance of assessing her figure, carriage, size and looks and reporting on them to the boy's parents when he returns.

*Chaila* is the term applied to a flirting boy, "a lad of the village."

89 GOING on the way, going on the way
Looking for a bride
Looking for a bride
Looking I was looking
Looking I was looking
For the bride in a thick cloth
For the bride in a cloth with flowers
I saw her, mother, at the spring
A perfect girl.

90 COLOURED *dhotis,*
Coloured *dhotis,*
Where have you been so long
After the sun has risen, *chaila?*

Scolding of the mother
Rebuke from the father
Loosing the young buffaloes
Took the time
Loosing the calves
Took the time.

In many Uraon villages a family of Ahirs (the cattle caste of Eastern India) is employed for tending the village herds. Their employment does not, however, exclude the Uraons from also tending cattle, and one of the usual occupations of young Uraons is to go with the buffaloes and cows into the jungle and see that none of them stray.

For "Ahir", see also Poems 97 and 98 and the notes to Poems 152 and 153.

In this and the succeeding poem the buffaloes are buffaloes but at the same time girls. Similarly, the calves are calves but also girls. "The cow of the mother" is analogous to the English phrase "the apple of the father's eye."

91 I CALLED you, I called you
In the morning
Coloured *dhoti*, coloured wrap
*Chaila*, where were you all the time?
The cow and the calf of the mother
Took the time
The buffalo and calf of the father
Took the time.

## (*b*) PRE-MARRIAGE: THE RIPE GIRL

92 WALKING, walking on the path, mother, I saw
The fig tree blooming, I saw the fig's blossom
A hundred blooms were smelling, mother, spreading for twenty miles
Over forty miles the blooms were smelling.

As soon as a girl becomes ripe for marriage the news spreads through the surrounding area like a scent.

With its prolific fruit, the fig is an obvious sexual and fertility image.

93 EVERY house has red *brinjals*
My own house has a small *brinjal*
Buy it, daughter of a vegetable seller
Hearing it, the tears fall.

A *brinjal* is a vegetable like the aubergine or egg-plant; and like the marrow is intended as a sexual image.

The vegetable seller is the Koeri, a member of the market-gardening caste. The daughter of the vegetable seller is here used as the relevant equivalent for the boy's agent—the person through whom the girl will be "sold". "The tears fall" because the girl's marriage will involve her separation from her family.

94 GREEN is the paddy, mother, green is the paddy
Green is the paddy, mother, and the parrots cannot leave it
Whose house has a ripe daughter, mother
On to that house, mother, the mind fastens
Inside that house, mother, the mind revels.

95 IN the decaying village, the sugar cane is planted
And who will say if it is sour or sweet
The daughter of the fallen Hindu cannot say
The daughter of the river man cannot say
In the decaying village the sugar cane is planted
The son of the casteman cannot say
The son of the neighbour cannot say
The daughter of the potter cannot say
The daughter of the casteman cannot say.

The sugar cane is the girl. The village is "decaying" partly by contrast with the girl's youthful vitality and partly because of the decline which will set in after she has left it. For the idea of the girl as the "life" of her family, see the note to Poem 5 and section (*f*) (1) "the death of the heart."

Just as Uraon parents always try to choose a boy and girl who will be compatible, the boy and girl always try to like each other after they are married, and in fact the majority of Uraon marriages strike the observer as happy. But obviously the data available to the parents are only very rough and general, and it is not until they have been living together for some time that a boy and girl really know each other. Even in England, where the opportunities for a couple to know each other before marriage are much greater, marriage advice harps on the unknown factors and the willingness to "give and take."

96 ON the high hills the bamboos grow
From a bamboo the blue bow is made
The shooting arrows are a spray of water
The gun is fired many rounds.

For "bamboo" as a girl symbol, compare Poem 126. Compare also T. S. Eliot, *Sweeney Agonistes*:

"Under the bamboo
Bamboo bamboo
Under the bamboo tree
Two live as one
One live as two
Two live as three
Under the bam
Under the boo
Under the bamboo tree."

Part of the force of this poem, based on a music-hall original, comes from the fact that bamboos with their bending curves have an obvious sexual reference and are thus a relevant background for the theme of the poem—"birth, and copulation, and death."

"The blue bow" is the ripe girl ("the bended bow of the body"—D. H. Lawrence). The arrows and the rounds fired from the gun are the ways in which the news of her ripeness is scattered over an area.

97 WHOSE cow, whose calf
Wander in the village streets?
The raja's cow, the rani's calf
Wander in the streets
Ahir, tie it, Ahir, bind it
Bind it with gold, tie it with silver.

98 WHOSE cow, whose calf
Wander in the village?
Ahir, tie them at the legs
Tie them at the neck
Tie them as gold
Tie them as silver
The Ahir has started
He has started to milk
The pot is shaking with the jets of milk.

The cow or calf is the girl, while the Ahir is partly her parent and partly her agent. "Starting to milk" means that the negotiations are in progress.

## (*c*) NEGOTIATION

### (1) THE SEARCH FOR A BRIDE

99 COME, brothers, we can see the lights and can go
On the four sides the lights go out
Now, brothers, we cannot go.

The lights are girls. The going out signifies that all the eligible girls have had their marriages arranged; so there is no longer any point in looking for a bride.

100 THE four brothers, the four brothers
The four brothers went away
The good riders on the red horses
Went to Bundu and Tamar.

A dispersal for the purpose of obtaining news of a suitable bride for whom negotiations can be opened.

### (2) THE ARRIVAL OF THE NEGOTIATORS

101 YOU planted a *munga* tree, father
The *munga* has spread its branches
The *munga* is in blossom
The bees hum and fly
They come to suck the honey.

In English poetry the honeysuckle is a constant symbol for "the ripe girl," and from classical times "bee" has been traditional for the suitor. Compare Rosalind's Madrigal by Thomas Lodge:

"Love in my bosom like a bee
  Doth suck his sweet:
Now with his wings he plays with me
  Now with his feet"

and Robert Herrick's poem *To Meadows*, which uses the symbol to ornament the object it symbolizes:

"You've heard them sweetly sing,
  And seen them in a round:
Each virgin like a spring,
  With honeysuckles crown'd."

A music-hall song which was popular at the end of the nineteenth century shows how these symbols have persisted and how wide is their appeal:

"You are my honeysuckle
I am the bee
I'd like to sip the honey sweet
From those red lips I see
I love you dearly
And I want you to love me
You are my honey honeysuckle
I am the bee."

For further use by the Uraons, see Poems 103 and 133.

102 I PLOUGHED with a brown bullock
I planted paddy
The paddy has ripened
The green parrot comes to steal
The sparrow comes to steal.

Here the paddy is the girl and the parrot and sparrow are negotiators.

(3) ATTEMPT AND OPPOSITION: THE DISCUSSION PROCESS

103 *Nanjani, manjani*
*Ranjani, manjani*
The bees murmur
The bees murmur
Give forty rupees, son-in-law
And the daughter is sold.

This relates to the discussion of the bride-price.

104 *Raimuni, patamuni*
The *mainas* fight and quarrel
The mango is in bloom
The *mahua* leaves have fallen
The *mainas* fight and quarrel.

*Maina*, usually a feminine symbol, here relates to the two troups of agents—the boy's and the girl's—meeting to decide the terms of a marriage.

105 IN the middle of the jungle, brother
The wild buffaloes stop the way
Run and shoot an arrow, brother
The sister does not listen.

"Wild buffaloes" are an image for a group of opposing relatives who in the last line merge with and become the sister who does not listen.

106 UNDER, under the hills
The spring has broken
There, mother, the cobras are moving
Mother, the cobras are moving
Cobra, I will cut you in seven pieces
Your blood will flow to the Jamna.

"Cobras" in this poem and in Poem 108 indicate the girl's parents, who are declining to accept the proposals of the agents. In the present poem "I" is the boy's agent who utters a mock threat in order to induce them to accept. The Jamna is a river in the Punjab which is usually paired with the Ganges. There is no evidence that the Uraons ever occupied territory as far north or had any direct contact with this river. As with the Gonds, who also use it as a poetic convention, it appears to have entered their geography through Hindu channels.

107 THE beating drum
The blowing trumpet
My lord goes to discuss a marriage
With your own relatives you block the water
On the bank of the Ganges
My lord goes to discuss a marriage
The small rain is falling.

Here a servant is speaking. "Block the water" means that the relatives oppose a proposal which but for their opposition would be accepted.

## (4) ATTEMPT AND SUCCESS

108 WITH bamboos the courtyard is bright
With a husband a girl shines
With fishes a net is bright
The seven rajas have merged in one

A single raja rules
Open the wooden door
We are hungry
We are thirsty
The two cobras raise their hoods.

In this poem "the seven rajas" are the negotiators who reach an agreement and so become the same as a single raja. As in Poem 106, the parents make a show of mock opposition.

## (5) ATTEMPT AND FAILURE

109 DAUGHTER, from a great distance I have come
and am thirsty
Daughter, why do you shut the door?
Why do you close the screen?
Father, I remembered the previous occasion
And so I shut the door, father
And I closed the screen.

This refers to a previous attempt at a negotiation which had failed.

110 THE shining river is not in flood
The son of the fisherman shows his strength
He sends the net in the wrong way
He throws a net and throws a second net
He catches snails and weeds.

"The shining river" is a symbol for the marriage market and the absence of flood is used to imply an absence of fishes. Compare the following Uraon poem:

Water of the tank flowing
Water of the well drying
The crowding fishes
Sport in the current.

In this poem the tank indicates a glut of girls, while the drying well means a scarcity of boys. The explanation for the failure is that the fishes or the girls are too few.

111 I WENT to collect leaves
By the tall rock and the deep pool I fished
As I am, father: so I shall stay—a bachelor.

### (6) THE SELECTED GIRL

112 UNDER the hills
From the clear springs the water flows
Water that the doves sip and the pigeons drink
In pairs they have come the wild geese
In pairs they have come
No. It is not the wild geese. It is not the doves.
It is the girl the elder brother chose.

In this poem the reference is to girls going to the spring to draw water. The wild geese come down in pairs in the same way as a girl and her girl-friend (or *juri*) go about together. Elder brothers not infrequently act as agents for the marriages of their younger brothers.

"Pigeon" is an obvious parallel image for an adult girl. In his article on the Nats, a caste of vagrant acrobats, Russell notes that "the Nat women are sometimes known as *kabutari* or pigeon either because their acrobatic feats are like the flight of the tumbler pigeon or on account of the flirting manner with which they attract their male customers."[1] Similarly,

[1] R. V. Russell, *Tribes and Castes of the Central Provinces*, vol. iv, p. 287.

Dalton notes their feminine emphasis in his note on the Juangs of Dekanal and Keonjhur in Orissa who have "a pigeon dance in which the arms of the girls are used as wings and the action of a love-making pigeon when he struts, pouts, sticks out his breast, and scrapes the ground with his wings is imitated."[1] As a pantomimic love image, a pigeon is a natural parallel.

"Dove" also has a wide usage in other countries as a love image. Compare Edmund Spenser, *Epithalamion*:

> "The whiles an hundred little winged loves
> Like divers-feathered doves
> Shall fly and flutter round about your bed."

and the following lines from a Chinese poem:

> "O dove, turtle dove,
> Do not eat the mulberries!
> O ladies, ladies,
> Do not take your pleasure with men."[2]

113 THE fawns frolic in the ploughed fields
No. It is not the *sambar*. It is not the barking deer.
This is the girl selected by the father
The bride chosen by the mother.

114 SOUTH of Bassia
In the twin tanks
A fish is living
No. It is not a fish
It is the bride selected by the mother
The bride chosen by the father.

1 Dalton, *Descriptive Ethnology of Bengal*, p. 156.
2 Arthur Waley, *The Book of Songs*, p. 96.

## (*d*) THE CLINCHING CEREMONY

115 DAUGHTER, give me water
Daughter, give me water
I come from a great distance, daughter, hungry and thirsty
There is no cup in the home
There is no vessel
Go, father, and drink the spring water
Go, father, and drink the stream water
I went to the spring, daughter, but the spring is dry
I went to the stream, daughter, but the dust is blowing
Sit on the verandah, sit at the door
The talk of the hundred days in a single day is over.

In this mock dialogue the demand for the girl is hidden in the demand for water. The girl knows that if she brings the water, and gives it to the boy's father, the act will betroth her. So she pretends not to understand, and by taking the thirst literally leads up to the exposure of "the bluff" with which the poem ends.

116 I WAS like a small fish, mother
No one looked at me
I played with a fan
I played with a basket
Mother, ten families are asking
Twenty families are asking
I was like a small fish, mother
I have filled the *lota* of water
I have brought the cups of water
Mother, ten families are asking.

The fan is a winnowing fan. The act of bringing the cups of water implies that the negotiations are over, and the twenty families are late.

117 THE spring water, mother
The spring water
The peacock drinks it
Gurgling in his throat
The cock drinks it
Tossing his head
The tiger drinks it
Biting with his mouth
The father drinks it
Minding his moustache.

It is characteristic of Uraons to dissolve the solemnity of an item of ritual by poking fun at the central figures; but only when the ritual is over and the heart is being warmed with drink.

118 THE deer graze on the slopes
The deer graze on the slopes
The deer graze
The fish sport in the pools
The fish sport in the pools
The fish sport
The bride sits in the mother's lap
The bride sits on the father's knees
The bridegroom catches fish
The bride jumps in the corners
Jumps, holding herself with glee, in the corners.

"Deer" and "fish" are symbols for marriageable girls.

There is no fishing ceremony in an Uraon marriage. "The bridegroom catches fish" would therefore mean that the marriage has been settled, a fish has been caught. The last two lines do not refer to any ritual exercise but to the girl's excitement at marriage.

## (e) THE MARRIAGE

### (1) THE APPEARANCE OF THE BRIDEGROOM

THERE is no special dress for the bridegroom and most families can afford only a new *dhoti*, a wrap and a turban. There is, however, a feeling that display is proper at a marriage, and if their means allowed, Uraons would doubtless approximate to the uniform described in the next two poems.

119 *Haire*, son-in-law, *haire*, son-in-law
Born a flower, son-in-law
*Haire*, son-in-law
How you glitter in the village
With shoes on your feet, rings on your legs
Bangles on the wrists, rings on your arms
Sash at the waist, charm on the chest
String at the neck, gold in the ear
Turban on the head
*Haire*, son-in-law
How you glitter in the village.

120 ON his feet he wore silver-coloured shoes
Where are his shoes today?
At his waist he put a silver-coloured *dhoti*
Where is his *dhoti* today?
He wrapped his body in silver-coloured clothes
Where are his clothes today?
On his neck he hung a silver necklace
Where is his necklace today?
He put on his wrists silver bangles
Where are his bangles today?
He tied on his head a silver-coloured turban
Where is his turban today?

These poems may be compared with an incantation employed by Lodhis, an agricultural caste of the Central Provinces. Before a Lodhi wedding starts the bride and bridegroom are given a doll made of dough with twenty-one cowries inside. The priest then climbs on to the roof of the house and commences to cry out:

"Are the king and queen here?" and a man below answers "Yes".

"Have they shoes on their feet?" "Yes."
"Have they bracelets on their hands?" "Yes."
"Have they rings in their ears?" "Yes."
"Have they crowns on their heads?" "Yes."
"Has she glass beads round her neck?" "Yes."
"Have they the doll in their hands?" "Yes."

And the priest then repeats the marriage texts and beats a brass dish while the doll is pulled apart like a cracker.[1]

## (2) THE ARRIVAL OF THE BRIDEGROOM'S PARTY

121 THE storks come down
In a long chain
In a long rope they come
On the banks of the Sankh and the Koel
In a long chain
In a long rope the storks come
On the banks of the Ganges and the Jamna
In a long chain
In a long rope they come.

[1] R. V. Russell, *Tribes and Castes of the Central Provinces*, vol, iv, pp. 116–117.

122 On the banks of the tank, mother
The grass is green
The grass is green
The geese and the small ducks have come
The geese and the small ducks have come
The son of the raja runs
The son of the raja runs, mother
He runs with a gun
He runs with a gun.

A gun is usually carried as part of the apparatus of a procession—but as a symbol of social standing and not for protection. A few ceremonial shots are fired. Most Hindu castes have a similar practice at weddings of letting off bombs and crackers.

123 Mother, I planted a mango tree
The mango grew and put out its spreading branches
On the eastern branch the pigeons perch
And the doves sit
The pigeons flock from twenty miles.

For "pigeons" and "doves", compare Poem 112. In the procession girls are as much a part of the bridegroom's party as boys are.

124 The cobra comes
With his hood raised
Asking alms
The heron comes
With his neck straight
Twirling his moustache
The frog comes
Diving and swimming.

"Asking alms" refers to the request for entertainment. The heron is the bridegroom and the frog is a revelling member of his party.

125 In the fields at Sissai
The bear does not eat paddy
The bear does not drink water
The bear comes
  The bear comes.

126 Bamboos you planted
The single bamboo you planted
The two you planted
The sparrows ask for shelter
The sparrows ask for lodging
The weaver bird sports with its feathers
The branches bend
The leaves shake.

127 The green parrot
The green parrot
The green parrot
Pretty the parrot
The raja on a *palki* and an elephant
Comes with the *diwan*.

128 Within the courtyard is the large elephant
Outside the courtyard is the blue horse
The son of the raja travels on the large elephant
The son of the *diwan* goes on the blue horse.

This is a magnified view of a procession—a fantasy version of the scale on which the Uraons would perform their marriages if they had the means of their Hindu landlords. In all the larger Hindu marriages one or more elephants move in the throng, and of recent years it has also become customary to take out a fleet of motor-cars. As a prosperity symbol the elephant dates from the Vedas.

For the purpose of his marriage a boy is magnified into a "raja" and his "best man" is termed the *diwan* or the raja's manager.

For "blue horse," see the note to Poem 152.

129 THE long foliage of the mango
The tiny leaves of the tamarind
The betel leaves
Are writing, mother
"The mother is coming
The father is coming
Coming with trouble
Coming with difficulty
Riding a pony
Tether the pony to a *nim* tree, father
Sit in the meeting
The uncle is riding an elephant
Tie the elephant to a plum tree, uncle
And sit in the meeting
The mother is coming
Put the basket under the eaves, mother
And sit in the meeting."

The basket contains the cloth for the bride-price.

130 MOTHER, put us up
Put us up under the slanting fig tree
Put us up, mother
We are the same caste as you, O mother.

131 SHELTER me, mother
Hide me
Hide me from the eyes of neighbours
The soldiers camp beneath the fig trees
Under the fig tree branches.

132 THE candles are ready
The seven carriers are waiting
The red gun is taken
The red box is borne
The scabbard and sword are going
The drums are beating
The red chair is carried
The dancers come
The bride's companion glitters
The tinsel flowers are bobbing
The tasselled switch
Reaches the ground
The horsehair plume
Brushes the earth.

## (3) THE MOCK CAPTURE

Concerning marriages among the Parjas of the Central Provinces, Russell writes that "the bride on going to the bridegroom's house to be married is accompanied only by her female relatives, no man of her family being allowed to be with her. This is probably a reminiscence of the old custom of marriage by capture, as in former times she was carried off by force, the opposition of her male relatives having been quelled. In memory of this, the men still do not countenance the wedding procession with their presence."[1] Similar ideas may explain the division of the marriage procession in Jashpur *thana* into two parts—the men going first but returning before the women come so that their association with the bride will not be evident. In this way the memory of marriage by capture may still persist, though not in the form of a pantomime but as an influence on the procedure. In the Mahuadan area mimic fights were occurring when Dehon wrote; and

[1] R. V. Russell, *Tribes and Castes of the Central Provinces*, vol. iv, pp. 375–376.

Dalton gives the following description, though it is not known to what area it applies. "When all is settled, the bridegroom proceeds with a large party of his friends, male and female, to the bride's house. Most of the males have warlike weapons, real or sham, and as they approach the village of the bride's family, the young men from thence emerge, also armed, as if to repel the invasion, and a mimic fight ensues, which like a dissolving view blends pleasantly into a dance. In this the bride and bridegroom join, each riding on the hips of one of their friends."[1] Mock capture in the form of a mimic fight probably still occurs in parts of Gumla subdivision.

133 THE bright and shining flutes
My brother has released the cattle
He fights with the bees, he fences with the bees
You, flute, must go to your mother
You, flute, will go to your father-in-law
In the four quarters of the night will your sleep come?
Flute, can your sleep come?

134 GET up, boy, get up
Release the brown cattle
Wait, mother; let the peacocks cry
Let the cock crow
Let the dew fall
And then I will loose the cattle.

In this poem the peacocks, the cock and the dew are symbols of marriage pomp—the decorations in the house prior to the wedding. "Releasing the cattle" means here as in the preceding poem the sending of the girl's party to meet the party of the bridegroom. "Fencing with the bees" refers to the mimic fight. Similar ideas are behind the next poem.

[1] Dalton, *Descriptive Ethnology of Bengal*, pp. 252–253.

135 Go I will, mother, go I will
I will go in the cold
I will go in the heat
Not caring for sleep
I will go with the few
I will fight with the many
I will go in the cold
I will go in the heat
Not caring for sleep.

## (4) THE WEDDING PRESENTS

Among Uraons the bride-price is frequently known as "the price of the milk"—the expenses which a family incurs in feeding, clothing and rearing a girl. It is a frequent argument in the marriage dialogues.

Besides the bride-price, however, it is conventional for a bridegroom to make certain other presents; just as in England there is the convention that a bridegroom should give a present to the bride's sister. The basis of the practice may be the submerged hostility which the act of removing the bride engenders and the corresponding need for a gesture to ease it.

136 SITTING high or low, son-in-law
The mother-in-law requires her present
The father-in-law will have the price of the milk
The grandmother asks for her *sari*
The brother of the bride desires his *dhoti*
The sister of the bride demands her gown.

137 IN Kesalpur we searched for a bride, mother
A bride coloured with spices
The father demands the marriage money
Where shall I find it?

The mother demands the price of her milk
Where shall I find it?
The brother demands a beautiful *dhoti*
Where shall I get it?
The sister demands some dancing feathers
Where shall I get them?

## (5) THE ANOINTING OF THE GUESTS

138 HUSBAND, your realm
Is the realm of *mahua*
The *mahua* blossoms
The *mahua* fruits
With a stick I pick them
In a little basket I gather them
In a tray I put them
In a bigger basket I keep them
On the head I load them
In the house I store them
On the stone I crush them
In the sun I dry them
In the pounder I husk them
With a fan I winnow them
In a basket I put them
With a hand I rub them
In the press I roll them
I catch the oil in a vessel
In the small pot I keep it
To the house I take it
With a rope I hang it
By a lamp I pour it
On the parents-in-law I smear it
Under and over I rub and smear them.

### (6) THE APPARATUS OF MARRIAGE

These poems are laments at the lack of marriages in a village. The scarlet powder is used for putting marriage marks on the boy and girl. The oil is for rubbing them or for mixing with the powder before it is applied.

139 SUCH a big village and no one meeting in it
*Hai hai* sister
The oil is left in the pot
*Hai hai* my sister.

140 SUCH a big village and no one meeting in it
*Hai daiya*
The pot, the scarlet still in the pot
The vessel, the oil still in the vessel
*Hai hai, daiya.*

### (7) THE EMOTIONS OF THE BOY AND THE GIRL

All Uraon boys and girls want to be married, but both sexes cry at the prospect of it. With girls the explanation is that marriage means a separation from their parents and a lonely process of adaptation in a strange household. Compare the Chinese poem:

On the hill is a clump of plum trees;
And on the lowlands, planted pear trees.
Not yet have I seen my lord;
With grief I am dazed.
What will it be like, what like?
I am sure many will forget me.[1]

[1] Arthur Waley, *The Book of Songs*, p. 75.

With boys the reason is partly a fear of the responsibility and partly a terror based on the unknown factors in the relationship. For both there is the tension of a crisis for which a natural outlet is in tears. In England a similar reaction is probably more usual than is acknowledged.

141 THERE the father of the boy is coming
My brother
Like the moon and the sun
Like the moon and the sun he is coming
The uncle of the boy is coming
Like the moon and the sun
Rise, girl, and bring the lamp
Rise, girl, and light the lantern
Like the moon and the sun
How shall I bring the lamp?
How shall I light the lantern
With sleep circling on the eyes?
The uncle of the boy is coming
The father of the boy is coming
The boy who must be married bitterly cries.

142 WHO are the spiders which have made these webs?
What are these webs, spider?
Bridegroom, your head is taken
Who has taken your head?
Bride, your eyes are filling
Why are you crying?

The spiders are here the negotiators.

143 MOTHER, for whom is the marriage bower?
Mother, for whom is this weeping?
For the son, mother, is the marriage bower
For the daughter, mother, is the weeping.

144 THE grinding stone turns slowly
Slowly the grinding stone turns
Sister sister
Slowly the tears fall
Slowly the tears fall
Boy boy
With the *dhoti* he wipes his tears
With the scarf he wipes his tears.

145 SHINING the rain falls
Below the plum tree the wet boy
Below the plum tree the wet boy
Heavy the tears fall
With the brother's scarf he wipes his eyes
With the edge of the sister's skirt he wipes his eyes.

146 VERY young the leaves I picked
And the leaves are put in the basket
Mother, the only brother
Bitterly weeps.

147 *Haire* the Sankh
*Haire* the Koel
Mother, the Koel river is in flood
The Sankh river is in flood
I grazed my cows by the river's bank
Mother, my calf is drowned
With a rope in her hands
And a pot on her head
The Ahir's daughter is crying, mother
The Ahir's daughter is crying.

In this poem there is a shift of images. The drowned calf is the girl lost through marriage. The Ahir's daughter is the girl weeping at being lost.

148 I WILL give you in marriage, I will give you in marriage, you say, elder brother
In a well I shall drown myself, elder brother
If you will pity me, you will take me out, elder brother
If you will have no pity, you will not move.

149 So long as I am in your house, elder brother
Your house will be like the feathers of the peacock
But when you will have given me in marriage, elder brother
Your house will be so silent that no one can say whether it is lived in or not.

## (8) THE DEPARTURE OF THE BRIDE AND BRIDEGROOM

150 THE water in the pool, mother
The water in the pool
The water in the pool is shining
The water in the pool glistens
The turtle rani in the palace
Goes with the otter raja.

151 IN the corn fields, in the wheat fields
Parrots from other sides have gathered
The parrot of the house has flown
The parrot of the house has flown to the jungle
Parrots from other sides have gathered.

152 MOTHER, my darling father my darling
The blue flag of the mother
Is stolen by a band
Is lost to a gang
Scour the villages
Scour the villages
O *mahtos* and *bandaris*
*Thikedars* and *subedars*
The blue flag of the mother
Is stolen by a band
Is lost to a gang.

"Blue"—in Europe and America blue is a symbol of death, depression and "eternal dolour". In Christian art it is used as a symbol for the Virgin Mary, and "blues" is an American negro term expressing a mood of depression. Compare the poem by W. H. Auden:

"For to be held for friend
By an undeveloped mind
To be joke for children is
Death's happiness.

Whose anecdotes betray
His favourite colour as blue
Colour of distant bells
And boys' overalls."

In contrast with this, in India "blue" is a vitality symbol. In Hindu usage it is the colour of Krishna, the god of love, and of the rain-giving god, Indra; and among the Uraons it is used to convey an attitude of admiration, a sense of shining splendour. There is a similar non-literal use in the poems of Ahirs, the cattle-tending caste of Bihar.

"The blue horse and the blue foal
And the blue mare with the golden bridle

On the blue mare rides Birnath, brother
Give me success tonight
And I shall shoe the hooves with gold."
(An Ahir poem of Shahabad district, Bihar.)

"Flag", which is here used as an image of the bride, is a common fertility symbol. Compare the Chinese poem:

"Your herdsman dreams,
Dreams of locusts and fish,
Of banners and flags.
A wise man explains the dreams:
'Locusts and fishes
Mean fat years.
Flags and banners
Mean a teeming house and home.' "[1]

[1] Arthur Waley, *The Book of Songs*, p. 168.

## (*f*) THE RESULTS OF MARRIAGE

### (1) "THE DEATH OF THE HEART," THE VILLAGE, THE FAMILY, THE GIRL

153 REARED in the mother's house, the *maina*
Has flown to the father-in-law
Has flown to the father-in-law, the *maina*
She is caught in a cage
She is caught in a cage, the *maina*
From birth she will stay the *maina*
To her death she will stay the *maina*
The mother's village is deserted, *maina*
The father's village is silent.

The image of the *maina* and the cage is also used in Bihar to symbolize the relation of the body and the personality. Compare the following Ahir poem from Harihargunj *thana*, Palamau district, Bihar:

"I fix my mind on God
Because he has made my cage
In the cage he has placed a *maina*
Ten doors has the cage
Bolted are nine and one is open
No one can say from where the cat will come
When God will let the *maina* fly
The mother will weep and beat her breast
The father will cry and strike his head
The wife will weep and tangle her hair
The neighbours will come and console her
And tell her 'Nothing is gained by crying
Who owned the *maina* has let it fly.'

I shall never have a husband as handsome as you
In a moment God made the cage
In a moment he has made it desolate."

154 THE nest of the white ant is graced by the cobra
The cobra is taken by the charmer
The nest is vacant
The river's pool glistens with the fishes
The big net is thrown by the boy who fishes
The pool is stagnant
The jungle sprang with the deer
The deer died in the trap
The jungle withers
The village lives in its boys
The bridegroom is taken to the spring
The village dies.

The taking of the bridegroom to the spring may mean the selection of the bride. There is no part of the marriage ceremony which involves his going there. Similarly, marriage will not mean his leaving the village, but simply that his time as a gay bachelor is over. "The village dies" in the sense that there will be less gaiety now that another boy has been married.

155 IN a tree are the red birds
Shot with arrows the birds fall
The tree is silent
In the jungle are the stags and does
Shot with a gun the stags die
The jungle droops
In the river's pool are the fish
Poisoned from a bush the fish die
The pool is stagnant.

Fish are caught sometimes with a line, sometimes with a net, sometimes by placing a basket in a small current, and sometimes as here by drugging a pool. W. V. Grigson, in *The Maria Gonds of Bastar* (p. 167), gives a list of the leaves, twigs and tree barks used by Bastar tribes for poisoning pools. He describes the process as follows: "The ingredients are pounded together with stones or axe-heads on a rock in or near the pool or tank; if the water is deep, they are thrown into it the night before the fish are collected; if it is shallow, the poisons act in an hour or two and can safely be thrown into the water in the morning. The fish are stupefied by them, and are easily collected floating on the surface."

156 THE fire catches the jungle
Where is my daughter?
Through the whole jungle I searched for her
Where is my daughter?

157 WHY, mango tree, the silent stillness?
Why, mango tree, the drooping branches?
In whose house I nourished a daughter
In his house are the drooping branches.

158 *Kahul kuta*, the *koel* calls
Sitting in the mango branches
*Koel*, you went away for twelve years
And in the thirteenth year you come and
gladden the grove.

Here the grove is the village and the *koel* is the girl returning after a long stay at her husband's.

159 In summer the jungle burns
All the birds leave the jungle
Dreadful the scene
With *asar* the rain begins
The bent branches grow
The birds come into the jungle
Beautiful the jungle.

160 The mud bungalow you built, father
The mud bungalow has fallen
Let it fall, mother, let it fall, father
When the Palkote water burns, I shall rebuild it.

In this poem the collapse of the house symbolizes the going of the bride. The implication is that nothing short of a radical change of heart will give the father the spirit to beget another daughter. At Palkote in Gumla subdivision there is a small stream which is famous for its coldness.

161 In the dew, the dew
I sowed the *rahar*
In the sun, the sun
The *rahar* withered
Living in the mother's house
Living in the father's house
Playing with the basket and fan.

162 Wood, you are cutting wood, mother
But the shoots will not spring again
Will never spring again
My mind is dying in the rocky uplands
Never will the shoots spring again.

Marriage means the cutting of the girl's connection with her parents, a severance of the affections which will not shoot again.

163 You brought me up, mother, you brought me up
You brought me up like a pet parrot
You brought me up like a tame *maina*
You have thrown me away, mother, you have thrown me away
You have thrown me away like a leaf platter and a leaf-cup
You have thrown me away like a bitter gourd.

Water bottles are made from gourds. If the gourd is bitter, the bottle is of no use and is thrown away.

## (2) THE DESTRUCTION OF FRIENDSHIPS

Except in the last poem of this section, *juri* does not necessarily mean the relation of a girl with a boy-friend, but more probably refers to the friendship between two girls. "Lived with" in the last poem does not necessarily mean that she was his mistress. Its equivalent could as well be "we used to go about together."

164 FROM where did the storm come
Which is taking away my *juri*?
From the east the storm came
And is taking away my *juri*.

165 MY mother sends me to the house of my father-in-law
*Juri*, I will stay here today and tomorrow
The following morning I will go away.

166 I AM going to my father-in-law, *juri*
And they scold me
They scold me
I am going to my father's house, *juri*
And they scold me
They scold me
Stay on the road, *juri*
The moon will shine, the flutes will play.

167 WHERE are you going, *juri*?
My *juri's* company is lost
Stay on the road, *juri*
The moon will shine the flutes will play.

168 TOGETHER we lived
Our *maina's* love is broken
The company of the *maina* is lost
On the path to the spring
Call and bring me the *maina*
Call and bring me the *maina*.

169 *Haire* the tie of the *juri*
Formed as we went to pick berries
*Haire* the tie of the *juri*
Formed as we went to draw water.

170 I LIVED with my girl
The enemy has taken her
Let the snatcher steal
Let the flier flee
Leave your care, brother
For you is a bride with a finer figure.

## (3) THE BRIDE IN THE HUSBAND'S HOUSE

171 THE tawny cow has left the house
Has gone to the forest
Tiger, don't eat it
O tiger, don't eat it
Born today, born only yesterday
Give milk to that calf.

172 WORK and you will get your food
And no one will scold you, mother.

173 OTHERS have a loving father-in-law
My father-in-law is bitter as the *karanj*
Go east go west
But never to the father-in-law.

174 DAY and night, the father-in-law sleeps
Father-in-law, I cannot sleep
Girl, do not lose heart
My son sits in the raja's *darbar*
Girl, my son sits in the rani's *darbar*.

175 No one no one, brother
No one in front of me, brother
No one behind me
Going and coming in my house
I am like a child with no parents
I am like an orphan.

176 WHEN I go to my mother's house, *juri*
My parents-in-law are cross with me
When I go to my mother's house, *juri*
My mother is angry.

177 THE grindstone turning
The thin legs parted
The mother-in-law scolding
The sister-in-law bickering
Listen, my mother
Listen, my father
The ten bones are shining
The twenty bones will whiten.

The meaning is that unless her parents-in-law treat her better the girl will kill herself.

178 YOU have married me, mother, on the banks of the river
Looking at the river I cannot sleep
What shall I do, daughter, what shall I do, son?
Your husband does not listen.

179 IN the jungle the peacock cries
By the spring the parrot calls
Parrot, do not call; hawk, do not cry
As yours is my sorrow
As yours is my fortune.

Compare the Chinese poem:

O Oriole, yellow bird
Do not settle on the corn
Do not peck at my millet.
The people of this land
Are not minded to nurture me.
I must go back, go home
To my own land and kin.[1]

[1] Arthur Waley, *The Book of Songs*, p. 95.

180 THE dove, the dove
Calls in the hills, the hills
I have no mother and I cannot sleep
I have no father and I cannot sleep.

181 THE brown doves gather in the hills
Hearing the dove, mother, I cannot sleep
Hearing the dove, father, I cannot sleep.

182 THE brown dove coos in the different hills
Dove, my mother is not here, I cannot sleep
Dove, my father is not here, I cannot sleep.

In these three poems the dove both parallels the feelings of the girl and is also the girl herself.

# DIALOGUES FOR URAON MARRIAGES

# DIALOGUES FOR URAON MARRIAGES

THE use of symbolic dialogues at the stage of negotiation is fairly common among the tribes of Central India. Among the Turis, a Hinduized offshoot of the Mundas, the bridegroom's ambassador announces his business with the phrase: "I hear that a sweet-scented flower has blossomed in your house and I have come to gather it." To which the bride's father, if the match be acceptable, replies, "You may take away my flower if you will not throw it away when its sweet scent has gone."[1] Among the Khonds "a proposal for marriage is made by placing a brass cup and three arrows at the door of the girl's father. He will remove these once to show his reluctance, and they will again be replaced. If he removes them a second time, it signifies his definite refusal of the match, but if he allows them to remain, the bridegroom's friends go to him and say, "We have noticed a beautiful flower in passing through your village and desire to pluck it.""[2]

An analogous method is used by the Gadarias, the occupational shepherd caste of Northern India, one of the ambassadors opening the conversation by saying, "We have the milk and you have the milk-pail; let them be joined." To which the girl's party, if the match be agreeable, will reply, "Yes, we have the tamarind and you have the mango; if the *panches* (village counsellors), agree, let there be a marriage."[3]

Roy records a similar use by Birhors when a party from the girl's house come to take the girl back to her parents a few days after the marriage. After they have settled themselves "they are asked by some elder of the bridegroom's *tanda*: 'Where do you come from? Where are you going?' They reply: 'We are come to these parts to look for strayed cattle. A herd of cattle had gone to our parts from this side. We had a she-calf. She joined the herd and came away in this direction.'

[1] R. V. Russell, *Tribes and Castes of the Central Provinces*, vol. iv, p. 590.

[2] ibid., vol. iii, pp. 467–468.

[3] Ibid., p. 5.

The first speaker replies: 'Look out for your calf then; find her out, see whither she may have gone.' 'Ah! here she is,' cries one of the bride's relatives. 'Well then,' is the reply, 'if she is your calf, you may take her home.' "[1]

The origin of these dialogues is partly in the wish for amusement—to cover the business with a film of fun; and partly in a sense of embarrassment—from the feeling that a girl's marriage is not a proper subject for higgling. This embarrassment is removed by the symbolism which retains the business nature of the talks but softens them by transferring the subject to an animal or a vegetable. In this way the brutality is removed while the business is preserved.

Of the symbols used in the three dialogues, marrow is a standard sexual image, its swelling growth being used to suggest both a ripeness for marriage and a pregnancy after marriage. In a similar way, in India as in Europe, a cow is a symbol for a woman. Deer becomes a feminine image by being an object of pursuit.

[1] S. C. Roy, *The Birhors*, pp. 206–207.

## THE DEER DIALOGUE

*A* (*leader of the bride's party*): Who are you and what are you doing here?

*B* (*leader of the bridegroom's party*): We are hunters and for many years have hunted in the deep jungles of Chota Nagpur. But until now we have never had any luck. Today we had all the trouble of the chase, but at the end of it we only wounded a spotted deer and it got away. We followed the trail of its blood, and the marks led us to this door. There can't be any doubt that the deer has run to cover here. Where is it?

*A:* No wounded deer came this way. We do not keep deer in our house.

*B:* But look at the blood on the door where the deer went in. Make it over to us.

*A:* You are speaking of a deer you wounded in the jungle. There isn't any wounded deer here; but it's true there is a pet deer of ours which we have had since it was a fawn.

*B:* The only deer we want is the one we shot. Are you sure that your pet deer hasn't strayed into the jungle and got shot?

*A:* We are always extremely careful to see that it grazes near the house. You must have shot some other deer and come here by mistake.

*B:* But with our own eyes we saw the deer actually run into the house. Possibly your own deer was grazing in the jungle and got shot by accident. But as it has taken one of our arrows, we cannot give it up.

*A:* You seem very sure of this deer. Can you describe it in any detail?

*B:* We didn't get too good a view of it, as it was off as soon as we saw it. We were lucky to hit it with an arrow; and after that the trail of blood brought us here.

*A:* That doesn't get us very far. It is quite obvious that you haven't shot our pet deer; and are trying to bluff. What was the age of the deer? And what was its colour?

*B:* As I said, we didn't get a good view of the deer; but it seemed to us to be full-grown and dappled in colour.

*A:* The description tallies with our pet deer, but would you be able to pick it out if we put it with some others?

*B:* Yes. We should know it again if we saw it—that deer which has brought us so far without any food or drink.

*A:* Then there is nothing more to say. It must have been our deer which you shot while it was grazing. And since you have shot it, we shall have to make it over to you. But remember that it has lived here ever since it was born, and we have had a good deal of trouble in bringing it up. Its mother was very rich in milk, and unless you have numerous fields and a large jungle it won't be happy with you.

*B:* Don't worry about that. It will be quite all right with us. There are several jungles close by and plenty of green pastureland. It will be able to go from jungle to jungle and field to field without any danger. We don't allow any hunters in our jungles. It will even be better off than it is at present.

*A:* There is something in what you say. But after all, the place will seem strange to it, and it may not like it. Still, since it belongs to you, we have nothing to say. Before we actually give it up, though, you should pay us back all that we have spent on it.

*B:* As we shot the deer with our own arrow, it obviously belongs to us. But we do not want to be unpleasant and take it without paying you your expenses. How much did you have to spend on bringing it up?

The bride-price is then discussed and the dialogue concludes.

*Gumla thana.* 1936.

## THE MARROW DIALOGUE

*A* (*leader of the bride's party*): Who are these strangers who have come to the house in the dark?

*B* (*leader of the bridegroom's party*): We are only some poor travellers who have nowhere else to go. From a great distance we have come, and now the journey has left us too weak to go any further. In the hope of getting our strength back we are thinking of resting for a few days in this lovely Chota Nagpur, and when we are fit again we shall make a new start. At the moment we are famished with hunger. We have a little rice and water but no vegetables with which to make curry. Everywhere we have been looking for vegetables but getting none. Now we have heard that in this house there are some marrows, and we have come to ask if you could spare us one.

*A:* What nonsense is this? Marrows in our house? This is the house of our ancestors in which we have lived for years, and never have there been any marrows in it. We do not understand how you can have heard of any here, and in fact from what you say it looks as if you are thieves who under the pretence of asking for a marrow have come to steal our property. Get out.

*B:* No, brother, we are not thieves. You ought not to speak so sharply to hungry or thirsty strangers. Very humbly we ask you to give us what we want. We are sure some marrows are here, as we saw them on the roof. There is a particular one on which we have got our eyes, and we are set on getting it.

*A:* I am very sorry, but you are quite mistaken. There are no marrows here. But we have got a little curry, and this we will gladly give you.

*B:* I am afraid a curry will not do. It is the marrow we want.

*A:* You seem unusually set on it. It is true that before the rains we sowed a few marrow seeds. The plants have now grown up and are bearing marrows—some of them full-sized, some half-sized, while others are still very small. But as they are all on the same stalk, none of them can be picked yet. Which was the marrow you wanted? Can you describe it?

*B:* The marrow we would like is on the corner of the roof and can be easily seen from outside. It appeared to us to be a quite unusually good one—very round and with not a single blemish.

*A:* I have not seen our marrows and did not know we had one like that; but it is certainly true that there are some marrows on the roof. Here is the largest which you must have got in mind, and a very tasty curry it will make.

*B:* You will excuse us, but the big one is not the one we want. It will only spoil the curry. The half-sized one is the one we are after.

*A:* I am very sorry, but we cannot possibly part with that. We are keeping it for chutney, and besides, in order to pick it, we should have to disturb the whole stalk.

*B:* The chutney does not matter, and we will pick the marrow so carefully that none of the other marrows are damaged. If you do not mind, we will go up and get it.

*A:* Since you are so keen on getting this marrow, we withdraw our objections. But we would point out that we have all along been growing it for sale. It has cost us a good deal of time, money and labour. When the plant was young, it had to be continually watered and watched. A special gardener had to be employed. Manure had to be given. We also had to take precautions against animals. Then when it grew taller a stick had to be put for training it on to the roof. Even then our troubles did not end. When the marrow itself began to form we had to keep a watch on it to prevent it from being stolen. You can imagine the bother to which we were put and will understand that we cannot just give it away for nothing.

*B:* We quite appreciate all the time and labour which have gone to growing it, and we do not want it for nothing. We are quite willing to pay a price.

*Gumla.* 1936.

# THE COW DIALOGUE

*A* (*leader of the bridegroom's party*)*:* Friends, we heard that one of our lost cows has come to your village and is in your cowshed.

*B* (*leader of the bride's party*)*:* Yes. There is a cow which has been in our cowshed for a long time. Perhaps you would know it if you saw it? Is it white, black, red or grey? Here are the cows.

*A:* Friends, we are in luck's way. That grey cow over there is the very cow which has been missing for a long time. Now we have found it. I am afraid we shan't be able to pay you anything for keeping it so long, but we will just take it away.

*B:* As it is your property, of course, we do not claim it. But we would like to know what happened while you were looking for it. And as it has been in our cowshed for so long, we shall naturally feel sorry at parting with it so quickly. But it obviously belongs to you, so what can we say?

*A:* You quite properly ask for certain information. And I shall try to give it. While the sun was rising in the east, the parrots were screaming together and were eating the ants in the *cheetka* tree. Twelve girls with newly washed hands and feet were coming from the spring in new clothes carrying fresh water on their heads. We stopped and had some banter with them. After that we met a royal youth who was bringing from a great distance his horse, elephant, *doli* and *palki*. Owing to this, the road was full of dust and the drums were rolling like thunder. We were able, however, to reach your house in safety—the thorns not pricking us and no lizard crossing the path, and no jackal howled. Just before we reached your house we saw a girl with a pot of water, and she went inside your door. In this way and without any accident we safely reached your house.

*B:* Father of the bridegroom, I am extremely pleased to hear you say it. You have come on a truly auspicious day. Good luck to you.

Gumla *thana*. 1936.

# OMENS

# OMENS

LIKE a belief in the influence of the stars, a belief in omens springs from a sense of the connectedness of phenomena. But unlike the stars, an omen itself does not influence a line of action. It merely indicates that a certain train of events is in operation and suggests the consequences if a certain line of action is pursued. Just as a piece of litmus paper tests whether a solution is acid or alkali, an omen tests the sum of circumstances at a particular time.

Omens are almost always general symbols of "life" and "death", "prosperity" and "failure"—terms to which all projects can ultimately be reduced. Consequently when a particular project is in hand, such as a marriage, a party has no difficulty in using the traditional symbol as a symbol of its particular case. And since the symbol is for the time being the object which it symbolizes, the appearance of the omen is easily taken to involve the future occurrence of the event. An omen is in fact a symbol of the future seen in the present, and for this reason it is able to act as a test.

Among the Uraons all omens are capable of this analysis.

## BAD OMENS

(1) A thorn pricking. This is a bad omen because it implies a wound which may mean a loss of blood and a corresponding loss of vitality; or alternatively because it implies a sore which will act as a check.

(2) A lizard. As a cold-blooded creature this is an "anti-life" symbol.

(3) An empty pitcher. This indicates an absence of water which from its life-giving powers is a normal "vitality" symbol.

(4) An empty-handed girl. The absence of property or wealth. Equals poverty.

(5) A woman carrying ashes or clothes in an earthen vessel. These are carried for washing purposes and symbolize weakness, as new clothes would symbolize strength.

(6) A dead animal being removed. The destruction of property.

(7) A snake in the path. A danger symbol.

(8) A vulture overhead. As a vulture feeds on carrion it tends to be associated with death. The fact that the vulture is overhead shows that it is waiting and that a death is imminent. The imminence rather than the actual occurrence of a death is bad; since once a death has occurred, death is temporarily out of the way.

(9) Hearing an owl. The owl's cry as in England suggests harm and horror.

(10) Hearing a jackal. As a jackal feeds on carrion, its cry has the same meaning as the waiting vulture. The howl indicates the temporary absence of death but its future possibility.

## GOOD OMENS

(1) A lamp burning. This indicates oil in the house and is a mark of prosperity.

(2) A woman carrying water. Compare the third bad omen.

(3) A raja or a royal youth. A power or a wealth symbol.

(4) A corpse being carried. This is a good omen because it indicates that death is out of the way.

(5) A jackal crossing from left to right. The left side is regarded as a centre of greater vitality than the right. Hence the jackal going from left to right means that the animal is going away from the life centre, and thus that a death symbol is being removed.

(6) Seeing monkeys in the path. This is possibly a semi-Hindu omen—monkeys being sacred, and their presence being thus the equivalent of a blessing.[1]

The Uraon belief in omens can perhaps be identified with the sense of subconscious non-logical relations which produces the images in certain of the dance poems. It could be said that the cow dialogue is a practical application of the image-systems of the poems.

[1] The first five bad omens and the first four good omens are current in Gumla *thana*. The remainder are noted by Dehon, *The Religion and Customs of the Uraons*.

# URAON MARRIAGE SERMON

## URAON MARRIAGE SERMON

I SHALL speak in riddles. In an ebony bush it looks to the sky. God is above and the elders are below. Attend, boy and girl.

Imagine you are out for hunting, boy, and you kill a deer. You will bring it home, and the girl will cook it. When she has cooked it, she will cut it up. But mark. For all others she must serve the flesh on a tiny tamarind leaf; but for herself she must take it from a large *korkot* leaf.

Attend again. When the bull is killed for meat, girl, you must insist on having the flesh, on having only flesh—nothing else. The boy will have the bones, nothing more than bones.

Then again. When on a hunting expedition, he slips in a ditch, laming his leg and losing the use of his fingers, never say, never say he has become a wreck.

And listen, boy. If your girl, going to pick leaves from the *koenar* tree, falls from a branch and breaks an arm or a leg, you must never say she has become useless. Never tell her she has lost the use of her hands.

As the fig tree gives many fruits, so you will have your children.

Rise and salute the elders.

Like the symbolic dialogues, the custom of a sermon is not confined to the Uraons but is shared with various Indian tribes. Mr. W. V. Grigson gives the following description of a sermon at a wedding of Maria Gonds in Bastar, Central India. "The two chains of girls suddenly opened out, leaving the bridegroom and bride together, and the girl's father and the bridegroom's elder brother were with them, holding their hands. The old father . . . held up his hand for silence, and started a long speech, asking the bridegroom's elder brother, 'Have you come willingly for this flower? Will you wear it and cherish it? It is fresh and tender, and will not bear rough handling. Know you how witless women are? If she be a poor housekeeper, pardon her. If she cook badly, pardon her. If she speak to other men, do not take it amiss but pardon her.' "[1]

Dalton gives a similar account of a sermon at a wedding of Santals in the Santal Parganas. "Oh boy! oh girl! you are from this day forth to comfort each other in sickness or sorrow. Hitherto you have only played and worked (as directed), now the responsibility of the household duties is upon you; practise hospitality, and when a kinsman arrives wash his feet and respectfully salute him."[2]

A sermon on somewhat brusquer lines is given to his son-in-law by the father of the bride at a wedding of Chakmas, a tribe in the Chittagong Hill tracts of Bengal. "Take her. I have given her to you; but she is not acquainted with her household duties. If therefore at any time you come back from the jhum and find the rice burnt, or anything else wrong, teach her: but do not beat her. But at the end of three years, if she still continues ignorant, then beat her, but do not take her life; for if you do, I shall demand the price of blood at your hands, but for beating her I shall not hold you responsible or interfere."[3]

Rai Bahadur S. C. Roy gives a Kharia marriage sermon at pages 265–266 of Volume One of his book, *The Kharias.*

## NOTES ON THE SERMON

"In an ebony bush it looks to the sky." This riddle is also used to preface the alternative version of the marriage sermon given at page 163, *Oraon Religion and Customs.* Roy states that the answer is *Asaglaro,* a kind of hairy insect which is poisonous.

The command to the girl always to take the larger share of a meal is perhaps based on a sense of the greater survival value

[1] W. V. Grigson, *The Maria Gonds of Bastar,* p. 256.

[2] Dalton, *Descriptive Ethnology of Bengal,* p. 216.

[3] Lewin, *Hill Tracts of Chittagong,* p. 70, quoted H. H. Risley, *Tribes and Castes of Bengal.*

of women for the tribe. It does not, however, appear to be an invariable instruction, as in Roy's version the boy and girl are told to eat the meat half and half, while in Dehon's account the girl is required to give the boy twice as much as herself.

Roy notes that "the inability of a wife to climb trees well is sometimes urged as a valid ground for divorce," as the leaves of several kinds of trees are eaten as vegetables and "it is one of the ordinary duties of a wife to gather them."[1] The Uraon horror of lameness amounts almost to hysteria. In one poem a man insists that he cannot live any longer with his woman as she limps in the right leg. The reaction is hysterical, not simply because a cripple is a burden but because the lameness cramps the village sense of exuberance.

For the reference to children, compare Psalm 128:

> "Thy children shall be as the fruitful vine upon the walls of thine house
> Thy children like the olive-branches round about thy table."

[1] S. C. Roy, *The Oraons*, p. 90.

# URAON FAREWELL ADDRESS

## URAON FAREWELL ADDRESS

A WOMAN is a man's weapon. With it he protects his house, his wife and children from his enemies. With this weapon is the deer killed and the meat cooked.

Today the most important thing to remember is that the girl whom we are now sending away for ever is like an arrow. When an arrow hits a living thing, it can never be got out before it has killed. In a similar way our daughter is going into your heart. Keep her in your heart always. The arrow which is made of iron takes life, but the girl who is like an arrow gives life. Only at death will this girl-like arrow issue from your heart, and until death it will stay in you. Farewell, the darling arrow. The man whom you longed to strike is hit. Farewell. For life we are leaving you. Cleave to him. Eat and drink with him. Be happy.

The conception of the bride as a man's strength is also expressed in a marriage poem where the bow is the girl.

183 WITH the small red bow
With the big red bow
He puts down the country with the red bow
He puts down the land
The country is your trust, red bow
Defend the land with the red bow
Protect the land with the red bow.

"Arrow" is possibly the most widely used marriage symbol in India. At the marriages of Gandas in the Central Provinces an image of a deer is made with grass and placed behind the ear of the bride. The bridegroom then throws a toy arrow at it made of grass or thin bamboo.[1] Among the Koltas an image

[1] R. V. Russell, *Tribes and Castes of the Central Provinces*, vol. iii, p. 15.

of a monkey or a deer is made of powdered rice, and the bridegroom is required to shoot an arrow at it—the image being brought back, cooked and eaten after he has done so.[1] Among the Kawars, a tribe living in the Chhattisgarh Hills in the Central Provinces, the bride and bridegroom return to the boy's house after the marriage, and the boy then shoots arrows at seven straw images of deer over his wife's shoulder, and after each shot she puts a little sugar in his mouth.[2]

There is an almost identical procedure among the Birhors of Chota Nagpur, except that the deer are omitted. Here the bride and the bridegroom perform a strange ambulation round the bridegroom's house. They begin by setting out for the bride's home—the girl carrying a pot of water, a little sugar and a basket of clay balls, while the boy carries a bow and arrow and a mango branch. When the girl reaches the limits of the boy's family area, she puts her burden down and darts away in the direction of her father's house. The boy then drops his bow and arrow and dashes after her. When he catches her, he beats her on the buttocks with the mango branch and brings her back to the basket. They then move back to the boy's house—the boy shooting an arrow towards it—and as they reach the place where it falls the bride gives, him sugar, washes his mouth and hands back the arrow. In this way the arrow is shot five times—the fifth time bringing them up to the house. In the house the bride and bridegroom take turns in throwing the clay balls at each other.[3]

The arrow plays a similar significant part in the concluding stages of a Munda marriage. Early in the morning of the day following the wedding "the bridesmaids, who with the young men have been merrily keeping it up all night with song and dance, burst into the nuptial chamber and bring forth the blushing bride and her bashful lord and their clothes. They all go to the river or to a tank to wash the clothes and bathe;

[1] R. V. Russell, *Tribes and Castes of the Central Provinces*, vol. iii, p. 541.
[2] Ibid., p. 394.
[3] S. C. Roy, *The Birhors*, pp. 203–204.

and parties of boys and girls form sides under the leadership of the bride and bridegroom and pelt each other with clods of earth. The bridegroom next takes a water vessel and conceals it in the stream or water for the bride to find. She then conceals it from him, and when he has found it she takes it up filled with water and places it on her head. She lifts the arm to support the pitcher, and the bridegroom standing behind her with his bow strung, and the hand that holds it lightly resting on her shoulder, discharges an arrow through the pretty loophole thus formed, into the path before her. The girl walks on to where the arrow falls, and with head erect, still bearing the pitcher of water, picks it up with her foot, takes it into her hand and restores it to her husband with a graceful obeisance."[1]

It is obvious that on one level these procedures are forms of pantomime which symbolize the bridegroom's duty as a husband—in the first cases as a hunter and in the latter cases as a protector. But it seems scarcely possible to deny them also the character of sexual symbols and not to regard the arrow and the deer, the arrow and the loophole as parallels for the sexual act. The arrow then becomes the equivalent of the male, and the object of the pantomime is to emphasize the sexual basis of the marriage. This aspect is given a further precision among the Khandaits and Savars of Orissa, where the arrow is actually used as a dummy bridegroom. In both these castes, if a girl arrives at adolescence without a husband being found for her, she goes through a form of marriage with an arrow. When the ceremony is over she widows herself by throwing the arrow in a river, but the seriousness of the ceremony is shown in the fact that if she ultimately gets a husband, she marries him in a widow's form.[2] At this stage an arrow is at once a weapon and a phallus.

In the farewell address the arrow is a "multiple" symbol acting both as a power image, to indicate the ways in which

[1] Dalton, *Descriptive Ethnology of Bengal.*

[2] R. V. Russell, *Tribes and Castes of the Central Provinces*, vol. iv, pp. 437, 505–506.

a wife helps her husband, and as a sexual image to denote their fusion. In the latter respect it resembles European usage—arrows or Cupid's darts being the symbols for the power of either sex to stimulate the other and the arrow being equally the effect of a woman on a man as of a man on a woman.

# URAON RIDDLES

# URAON RIDDLES

"An image is not striking because it is brutal or fantastic, but because the association of ideas is remote and exact. . . . A striking image, one new to the mind, is produced by bringing into relation without comparison two distant realities whose relations the mind alone has seized."

JACQUES MARITIAN, *Art and Scholasticism.*

URAON riddles are often brutal and fantastic, but their aim is to provide ordinary objects with remote and exact associations—to make images which will either startle with their vitality or amuse by their oddness or accuracy.

In many the method of construction is comparable to the first verse of the Sans Day carol:

"Now the holly bears a berry as white as the milk
And Mary bore Jesus who was wrapped up in silk."

A parallel in Nature is found for an action—the holly bears a berry as Mary bears Jesus—and this is intensified by a visual detail—the berry with its white skin standing for the child in its silk. In Uraon riddles a similar visual parallel is often the basis of the riddle.

In another type the image is a rational construction, as for example "the boy with the hundred eyes behind." This riddle starts with an analysis of the peacock emphasizing the "eye" marks on its tail feathers. Eyes are then taken as an image for the marks, while a boy is used as an image for its sex. In this way a fantastic image is constructed—an image which has no existence in ordinary life, but is composed of certain vital fragments. In recent paintings by Picasso there is a use of a somewhat similar method to create forms which alarm with their composite vitality.

A few riddles are simple exercises in analysis. An object or an action is analysed into its qualities and a positive quality is paired with a negative. An arrow, for instance, is analysed into

Go it can but come it cannot.

Alternatively, two positive but contrasting qualities are used as a summary analysis:

Coming it bends
Going it straightens

indicating the two contrasting characteristics of the pole which is used for lifting water from a well.

Certain traditional English riddles are clinched with a taunt.

"The land was white
The sea was black
It'll take a good scholar
To riddle me that." (Paper and ink)

In Uraon riddles this method is not often used, but the following is an example:

In colour like spice
And shaped like a *lota*
Who cannot tell this
Is the son of a monkey. (A bel fruit)

As a result of the mass literacy of the nineteenth century the petty cleverness of the play on words has come into English riddles.

Why did the bulrush?
Because it saw the cowslip.

In Uraon riddles there is hardly any reliance on verbal play, almost the only instance being in the following. "Some strings went into the water, but none of the strings were singed." This refers to a fishing net and the play of words turns on the use of "jal" in "jal" (water) and "jalna" (to singe or burn).

As a primary object of Uraon riddles is to give amusement, the occasions on which they are used are almost always marriage parties, when the guests are sitting round and whiling away the gaps between the ceremonies. A skill in putting and answering riddles is taken as an index to the skill of the two houses. Apart from this, riddles do not have any practical use.

There is, however, a small group of "kennings" or summary riddles which the Uraons use at night as substitutes for the names of certain animals—"a rope" for a snake, "the long-tailed one" for a tiger, "the woolly-coated one" for a sheep.[1] These are used as substitute counters in the same way as a cow, a deer and a marrow are used as symbols for the bride in a marriage dialogue. The use arises from the tabu against using a correct name after dark—the tabu springing from a sense of the identity of a thing and its name, and the apprehension that to name an animal may either cause it harm if it is a domestic one or cause it to do harm if it is a wild one. For the Uraons such "kennings" or summary riddles are as useful as insurances and as important as a gun or a club.

## A

1 The moon sizzles in the centre of a tank.

*A* chapatti *in a pan.*

In a tree on an anthill is the nest of a bulbul.

*A hookah.*

A white umbrella stands in a field.

*A mushroom.*

In a small pond is a flashing stork.

*A country lamp.*

A burnt rat makes a hole in the ground.

*A coulter.*

A curved deer has teeth in its belly.

*A sickle.*

[1] S. C. Roy, *The Oraons*, p. 361.

A tiger roars as it pulls a creeper.
*A handloom.*

A raja has a hoof on his knee. *A grasshopper.*

A white goat jumps over a fence.
*Ashes being thrown.*

A parrot plays on the dry stump of a tree.
*An axe.*

In a white field are the black seeds.
*Paper and ink.*

A cow gives birth to a bone and the bone gives birth to a calf. *A hen and an egg.*

There is only grass on the top of the mountain.
*Hair on the head.*

The white storks dance in the pond.
*Maize frying in a pan.*

A mouse frolics between two fences.
*A weaver's shuttle.*

A bird drinks with its tail.
(a) *A lamp.*
(b) *Grass.*
(c) *A well.*
(d) *A tank.*

The glinting fish raises a mound.
*A needle making a seam.*

A ghost speaks from a dry piece of wood.
*A gun.*

A kid springs between two mats. *A weaver's shuttle.*

A headless goat gapes at the sky. *Paddy stubble.*

A mint leaf sits on a swaying head.
*A cobra.*

An old woman knocks a white hen down.
*Snot.*

The goat sits while the string grazes.
*A marrow and its tendrils.*

In the belly of an elephant the *mainas* chirp.
*A house with children.*

A boy goes to his father's house. *A river to the sea.*

A stray cow grazes on an anthill. *A razor.*

A small cow gives a stream of milk.
*Mustard.*

A small bird dries up a pool. *A lamp.*

A dead cow breathes. *A pair of bellows.*

30 A dead sheep goes to drink water.
*A fishing basket.*

The belly of a mangy dog tastes sweet.
*A jack fruit.*

A fish sports in a drop of water. *The tongue.*

A spreading tree has a small bell. *Gram.*

An old barber has a house with no doors.
*A silk cocoon.*

A young goat roams from door to door.
*A grain measure.*

A black goat grazes on a black hill.
(a) *A tail.*
(b) *A razor.*

A small kid has a feather in its belly.
*A mahua flower.*

The red flag flutters once a year.
*The flower of the cotton tree.*

A pebble roves the world. *A pice.*

40 A brown cow lows in the middle of a field.
*A drum.*

A rotten sheep goes to bathe in a river. *Clothes (mixed with ashes for washing)*

On a mango tree is a red wrap. *A chillie.*

A cotton tree looks to the sky and has only one joint. *Durhi* grass.

A boy with itches goes to a raja's palace. *A jack fruit.*

The tall woman gives birth to a child through her head. *A plantain tree.*

A pretty thing destroys Ceylon. *Matches.*

A pony drinks water. *A lamp with oil.*

The father adds thorn to thorn and the mother revives the dead. *The father repairs the thorn-bush hedge while the mother transplants paddy seedlings.*

A dish sinks in a tank. *The moon.*

50 A slaughtered kid jumps over a roof. *Thatch.*

The sifter of the water has only one corner. *A lotus leaf.*

The hanged and buried enemy is coming. *A drum.*

The *champa* blossoms in a small tank. *A candle.*

A withered broom waves above a blackberry. *A goat's tail over a goat's dropping.*

A heated mouse runs to earth. *A coulter.*

An old man washes at sunrise and jumps on a horse. *A cooking pot.*

The black feather of a white line goes from house to house. *A letter.*

A dwarf with a long beard shakes his head. *Needle and thread.*

A dumb girl from the jungle makes water on the food. *A lemon.*

60 The old cripple eats salt. *A tamarind.*

A hundred rupees are in a red case. *Chillies.*

## B

A hut on the slope of a hill. *A nose.*

An earthen pot on the head of a sahib. *A solar helmet.*

A hundred creepers in a single spot. *A market.*

A thousand candles in a dish. *Stars.*

A white flag in the jungle. *The life-and-death tree.*

A red flag in the forest. *The cotton tree.*

A single leaf in a single tree. *A flag.*

A nest in a stump. *A* chelum.

70 A stone in the middle of a hill. *The ear.*

Herons in a pond. *Children in a park.*

A marrow without a stalk. *An egg.*

A gourd without a root. *An egg.*

Rice without a skin. *Salt.*

A root without a plant. *A puff-ball.*

A creature without a nipple. *A hen.*

A bamboo without a joint. *A hair.*
A pack-bullock that cannot be driven.
*A tiger.*
A blossoming flower that cannot be plucked.
*The sun.*
A fallen plough-stick that cannot be picked up.
*A snake.*
Two rolling pins on the slope of a hill.
*A woman's breasts.*
A finger in the stomach and a stone over the head.
*A ring.*
The bad-tempered mistress of a smartly smeared house. *A wasp.*

## C

The boy with the sickle. *A dog with a tail.*
The boy with the hockey stick. *A dog with a tail.*
The boy with the five eyes. *A flute.*
The boy with the four legs. *A cot.*
The boy with the hundred eyes behind.
*A peacock.*
The boy who makes the round turban.
*Rice while being boiled·*
The boy who knocks a man down.
*Rice-beer.*
The boy who only speaks when beaten.
*A drum.*
The boy who ploughs without hands or feet.
*A freshwater mussel.*

The bashful girl who stays behind.
*A comb in the hair.*

The girl who closes the door at the sight of a stranger. *A snail.*

The servant girl with her nipples behind her.
*A winnowing fan.*

The tall girl with her anus always open.
*The strings of a carrier's load.*

The man with eyes on his back. *A crab.*

The man with his house on his back.
*A tortoise.*

The man who orders without knowing.
*A corpse.*

The two brothers who sit together but never look at each other. *The eyes.*

The woman who bears a single child.
*A plantain.*

100 The woman who passes a powdered stool.
*A grindstone.*

The beautiful woman who blows from time to time. *A pair of bellows.*

The twisted woman who eats mud.
*A snail.*

The mother and daughter with the same name.
*Mahua and its flowers.*

The old woman who only eats wood.
*A cooking range.*

The old woman who hides her curry behind her.
*A bamboo fishing trap.*

The old woman with a mouthful of toothbrushes.
*A fireplace.*

The old woman who eases herself as she eats.
*A grindstone.*

The old woman who wears a heap of clothes.
*A hen.*

The crippled old woman who clears the jungle.
*A sickle.*

The tree with the honeycomb. *A* karanj *and its fruit.*

The tree with combs for the hair.
*A castor.*

The tree with the clods of earth.
*A jack fruit.*

The tree with the parched rice. *A castor tree in flower.*

The tree with the needles. *A jack fruit.*

The tree with the sickles. *A tamarind.*

The tree with the sticks. *A laburnum.*

The tree with the drums. *A jack fruit.*

The tree with the sweets. *A* bahra *tree.*

The *sal* tree that shakes without a wind.
*The tail of a dog.*

A small dove with a round belly.
*A* pan (*betel nut*).

The little bird with the head of meat.
*A* bhelwa (*a jungle fruit*).

The dove with its head on one side.
*A rafter.*

The bird with life in its hip. *Grass.*

The hen that lays a hundred eggs as it goes.
*A machine.*

The hundred crows with their heads on one side.
*The beams of a house.*

The animal with the two tails. *An elephant.*

The animal that lives in a black jungle and drinks red water. *A louse.*

The small horse with a hundred ropes.
*A weaving machine.*

The horse with the fourteen legs that quarrels as it goes.
*A pregnant woman riding on a pregnant mare counts up the possible legs, including those of her husband.*

130 The lame mare with the twenty-five fetters.
*A spinning wheel.*

The cow with one horn that feeds on its master's food. *A grindstone.*

The tigress with the empty belly and the pregnant tail. *An ant.*

The water that springs from a dry stone.
*Sweat on the brow.*

The spring that cannot bear a spark.
*The eye.*

The flower that shuts by day and opens at night.
*A mat.*

The white sandalwood that fades at once.
*Hail.*

The banyan leaf that stops where it fell.
*A footprint.*

The white flag that flutters once a year.
*Thatching grass.*

The big turban that stands on one leg.
*A wheel on its axle.*

140 The bamboo with the single joint.
*A snail.*

The stick of the brother-in-law which can only be got with a knife. *A dog's tail.*

## D

Handsome the son
Sagging the mother. *A marrow.*

Flat the mother
Thin the son. *A currystone and roller.*

Thin the mother
Plump the children. *A cotton tree and its fruit.*

Rough the mother
Smooth the children. *The outside and inside of a jack fruit.*

Bitter the mother
Beautiful the daughter. *The wild plum.*

Dirty the mother
Clean the daughter. *A brinjal.*

Bowels out
Blood within. *A rice bale.*

Big when born
Small when old. *A plough.*

150 Outside pretty
Inside empty. *A drum.*

Young and separate
Old and joint. *The flowers of a grass.*

Put down silent
Picked up noisy. *A drum.*

Little the eyes
Big the ears. *An elephant.*

Slippery the tree
Crooked the child. *A plantain.*

Little the garden
Beautiful the flower *A candle.*

Dirty the bark
Sweet to eat. *Honeycomb.*

Above the nest
Below the egg. *A* mahua *flower.*

Soft while unripe
Hard when it ripens. *A pot.*

Held in the hand
But not in the house. *An umbrella.*

160 Fire above
Water below. *A hookah.*

Twelve years old the goat
Single the piece of meat. *A snail.*

Neither root
Nor branch. *A fungus.*

Go it can but come it cannot. *An arrow.*

Kick it and it jumps.
*A rice pounder.*

Quickly it goes
Quickly it comes.
*The eye.*

Here it comes
There it goes.
*The eye.*

Dry going
Wet coming.
*A water pot.*

Eat it can but drink it cannot.
*A white ant.*

Catch one
Know all.
*Rice while being boiled.*

170 Going it bends
Coming it straightens.
*A saw.*

Coming it bends
Going it straightens.
*The pole of a well.*

Coming it whirls
Settling it lies still.
*The flower of a* sal *tree.*

Lying one colour
Going different colours.
*Eggs and chicks.*

Clenched fists coming
Open hands going.
*Birth and death.*

The white hen scatters them
The black hen gathers them.
*Day and night.*

The father murders it
The mother saves it.
*A bunch of paddy seedlings.*

Sunrise wants one brother
Sunset wants the other. *The mat for sleeping: the pole for hanging clothes.*

The black cow is sleeping
The red cow is licking. *A black pot on a fire.*

## E

A man makes money by burning what he makes. *A potter.*

180 Two boys squeeze a couple of girls to make them pass water. *An oil press.*

The ten crooked brothers have no head and the belly is the mouth. *A crab.*

A girl tidies a room and goes to the back of the house. *A comb.*

The son of the raja cannot bear pain. *The eye.*

A man goes out to see the world and a dwarf stays behind. *A footprint.*

A brown bullock feeds on branches and dies when it drinks water. *Fire.*

The body of the elephant is inside but its tail is outside. *A needle and thread when sewing.*

A bent old man is wanting salt. *A tamarind.*

It raises a fishing rod and an ant's nest falls. *A bullock's dung.*

Slaughtered the goat and its blood bespatters two stones. *A louse between two nails.*

190 A stone on a smell and a pice on a stone, and a palace built without water. *An anthill.*

A cup on a cup and the son whiter than the father. *A coconut.*

Earth above and earth below and in the middle a painted pebble. *A* kesair *nut (which is found in the ground).*

Storks in front, a beak in the middle, a thief behind. *A man ploughing with two bullocks.*

Two wooden planks that neither fall nor come together. *The earth and the sky.*

Many bells that ring, but inside is a cake of wheat. *Bees in a honeycomb.*

Four legs in the morning
Two legs at noon
Three legs at night. *Childhood, manhood, old age.*

A jack-of-all-trades, but no one can hold him. *Fire.*

Many grind but one collects. *The teeth and the tongue.*

Neither in the bazaar nor in the town is it found. Peel it and it has no skin. Eat it and it has no stone. *A hailstone.*

200 With one ear of corn the house is full. *The flame of a lamp.*

Two on their backs and one on top of them. *Tiles on a roof.*

One rider and two horses. *A cooking range.*

The flower that opens in the rain and closes when the rain is over. *An umbrella.*

The son who is born before the father. *Smoke before flame.*

One who hears without ears *A frog.*
One who sees without eyes *A snail.*
One who moves without legs. *A snake.*

Go if you must, but twist your ear as you go.
*Padlocking a door.*

Who can measure a raja's *dhoti*? *A road.*

Water of two colours in a single pot.
*An egg.*

One likes rain *A farmer.*
One likes shine. *A washerman.*
A third likes talking. *A shopkeeper.*
A fourth likes silence. *A thief.*

210 Theft in the hair
Trial in the hand
Death between the thumbnails. *A louse.*

Seven holes in a single thing. *The head.*

Although it has no flesh, it lives. *A leech.*

It came out like a needle
It spread out like a hill
It left the body
It stuck in the nose. *Stools.*

Two goats are slaughtered for a stranger. The stranger has no teeth, and the goats have no bones. *A new-born child being breast-fed.*

Young, no one noticed me. Grown up, everyone takes off my clothes. *A maize cob.*

Everything will be burnt, but the stick of the cowherd will not be burnt. *A path.*

A house went into a pit. If the house grows, the inmates will go from field to field.
*A pit gets filled with water and the fishes come out into the fields.*

Tiny fishes gather when the dry tree is beaten.
*Children and a drum.*

Pole in one village
Pipe in another
Fire in a third
Smoke in a fourth. *A hookah.*

220 The house escapes while the inmates are caught.
*Catching fish with a net while the water drains out.*

See how active she is, but feel her and she has no pigtail. *A grain measure.*

Folded when the guest gets up. *A mat.*

Four brothers who stagger while a fifth waves a switch. *A cow and its tail.*

Of one colour, the parrot; but eaten, many colours. *A pan (betel nut).*

Two owners for each of the four co-wives.
*A cot.*

The head of a tired hen is cut with a knife, but it goes on walking. *A pencil.*

The black cow scares while the brown calf runs.
*A gun.*

Three heads with ten legs in a mixed village.
*A man driving a bullock cart.*

The brown cow invites, but the crooked cow scares. *Plums and thorns on a plum tree.*

230 Handled, it cuts twenty, but at times it licks a stone. *A razor.*

A cart without wheels looking for legs. *Shoes.*

Big-headed but not an elephant
Thin-waisted but not a leopard
Digs a hole but is not a mouse
Climbs a tree but is not a snake.
*An ant.*

# APPENDICES

# APPENDIX I

## BIOGRAPHICAL NOTES

(1) COLONEL E. T. DALTON. *Descriptive Ethnology of Bengal*, Calcutta. Office of the Superintendent of Government Printing, 1872, pp. 245–263. Section on Uraons. The first and the best short account of the tribe.

(2) SIR W. W. HUNTER. *A Statistical Account of Bengal*, Volume XVI, *Districts of Hazaribagh and Lohardaga*. Compiled by Sir H. H. Risley. Trübner and Co., London, 1877, pp. 279–296. Section on Uraons. The article on Uraons is based on excerpts from Dalton, but in certain places is misleading owing to incomplete quotation.

(3) SIR H. H. RISLEY. *The Tribes and Castes of Bengal*, Calcutta. Bengal Secretariat Press, 1891. Volume II, pp. 138–150. Article on Uraons. Differs little from No. 2, except in its statements concerning pre-marital morality.

(4) REV. F. HAHN. *Khurukh Folk Lore*, Calcutta. Bengal Secretariat Press, 1905. Contains a collection of Uraon folk tales and about two hundred Uraon poems in the original Uraon.

(5) REV. P. DEHON, S.J. *The Religion and Customs of the Uraons.* Memoirs of the Asiatic Society of Bengal, Calcutta, 1905. Relates to the area centring in the Mahuadanr *thana* of Palamau District, and as an account of *this area* is vivid and valuable.

(6) RAI BAHADUR SARAT CHANDRA ROY. *The Oraons of Chota Nagpur*, Ranchi, 1915. With No. 10, the fullest existing account of the tribe and a mine of fascinating details. Suffers from a tendency to over-generalize and does not particularize any of the areas to which it refers. Is of major importance for a knowledge of the tribe.

(7) R. V. RUSSELL, I.C.S. *The Tribes and Castes of the Central Provinces*, Macmillan, 1916. Article on Uraons. Volume IV, pp. 299–321. Contains useful excerpts from 3 and specially from 5.

(8) Sir M. G. Hallett, I.C.S. *Bihar and Orissa District Gazetteers, Ranchi.* Superintendent of Government Printing, Patna, Bihar, 1917. Contains a useful summary of the agrarian troubles and a brief note on Uraon customs.

(9) L. S. S. O'Malley, I.C.S. *Bihar and Orissa Gazetteers; Palamau.* Revised edition by P. C. Tallents, I.C.S. Superintendent of Government Printing, Patna, Bihar, 1926, pp. 54 and 60–61, give some short notes on Uraons.

(10) Rai Bahadur Sarat Chandra Roy. *Oraon Religion and Customs*, Ranchi, 1928. See No. 6.

(11) Rev. A. Grignard, S.J. *Hahn's Oraon Folk-lore*, Patna. Superintendent of Government Printing, Bihar, 1931. Obtainable in England at the Office of the High Commissioner for India, India House, Aldwych, W.C.2. Price approximately 7s. 6d. A revised edition of No. 4, containing most of the original material (but reducing the number of poems to twenty). Includes an English translation of the greater part of the contents. The translation is in a racy pseudo-English not without its charm. It should be noted that the twenty poems which Hahn correctly entitled "Songs for the May-June *jatra*" are fancifully interpreted by Grignard as a single ballad. Apart from the fact that they are all *jatra* poems, there is not in actual fact any connection between these poems, and any or all of them can be and are sung in any order. There are no Uraon ballads in the sense of long narrative poems containing a number of stanzas or of the type as pieced together by Grignard.

# APPENDIX II

# URAON DANCES

## NOTES ON THE DANCE-FORMS

WITH the exception of dances at *jatras*, the Uraons always dance to the rhythm set up by the drums. It is to this rhythm that the dance poems are fitted, and it is this rhythm rather than the actual steps which makes one dance differ from another. While the steps follow local variations within the tribal style, the drum rhythm of a dance is probably constant throughout the Uraon country.

The following notes are based on dances at Mandar and in Jashpur *thana*. They describe the steps of the dances as I saw them in December 1938 and are fairly typical of the same dances in Gumla subdivision. But the notes are not a general description and do not necessarily apply to dances in other areas.

### (1) "FESTIVAL" DANCES

(*a*) *Sarhul*.—The *Sarhul* dance in Jashpur is a series of fierce rhythmical jerks ending in a triumphant yell. The boys and girls form a curving line on the circumference of an imaginary circle and start by walking round hand in hand. As in all Uraon dances, the first movement is anti-clockwise. The leader who is usually a boy sings the *or* of the dance poem and the line clinches it by taking six jumps backwards on alternate feet. The line then moves into a rapid advance—starting with a step by the right foot, followed by a swinging pace by the left and ending in a jump forward with both the feet. By repeating this action, the line swings grandly round the circle.

(*b*) *Karam*.—In the *Karam* dance in Jashpur the girls form a parallel line behind the boys and both lines face inwards on the circle. The steps of the *or* begin by moving the right leg forward to the right and bringing the left leg behind it to a position slightly to its right. The right leg then takes another step to the right, and this is followed by a short step by the left. On every second step the beat is slightly emphasized by a bending of the torso, which is sometimes developed into a swinging stoop. The *kirtana* is a recoil from the decisive advancing of the *or* and consists of a swaying zigzag walk. The dancers incline to the right and go back round the circle in a loose swinging line. The transition from the *or* to the *kirtana* consists of a syncopated step in which the right leg is tossed forward, and before it touches the ground a slight hop is made by the left leg. The right foot is then brought down and the two feet jump back together. This movement is duplicated and a pace taken forward for the return to the *or*.

In the standard *Karam* dance at Mandar, as at Jashpur, the boys and girls form two curving lines on the rim of the circle, and the dance then consists of a zigzag walk to the right with the torsos erect, followed by a zigzag walk to the left with the dancers leaning forward. In the latter movement the emphasis is on every step by the left leg, the left foot being brought down firmly with a bend of the knee while the right leg is brought lightly back behind.

In a version known as the *Jugia Karam* at Mandar the boys and girls form two parts of a curved line half facing the centre of the circle. The boys are strung out in a loose line holding hands, while the girls interlock their arms and stand with their bodies touching. The line then moves round the circle, the girls walking smoothly while the men proceed with loose leaps. After an erect zigzag progress they move backwards, and then do a figure of four movements before the walk is resumed. This consists of two paces forward, first with the right leg and then with the left; the right foot then moves up to just behind the left, and the left is then brought back to a pace behind the right.

At Jashpur a brisker variant of the *Karam* dance called a *lujhki* is also danced. In this the movement is to the right and there is no reverse. The action consists of two figures each with four movements, the rhythm rising and falling round the third movement of each figure. In the first a pace forward is taken with the left leg and the right foot is swung forward for the second movement and brought on to the ground for the third, each movement being equal. The left leg then moves slightly left. In the second figure the right leg is brought with a swaying pause to the right, the pause accounting for one movement while the second brings the foot to the ground. The left leg then comes across in front of the right foot, and with the fourth movement the right foot takes a pace back. These two figures are then repeated, and in this way the dance moves round the circle. The dance is done with the knees partly bent and goes rapidly with a running swing.

(2) "JATRA" DANCES

(*a*) *Jatra*.—For the *jatra* dance at Mandar the boys and girls form a single line half facing the centre—the boys strung out among the girls, the right hand holding the left arm of the dancer in front. The line then moves round the circle in a swinging walk coming to a stop on the yell "*hurur*". A movement consisting of a pair of jumps is then taken, a pace back being followed by a jump with both the feet and a step forward being clinched with another jump. The line then resumes the walk. A variation of the step consists of facing inwards when the line stops, hopping with the left and then stamping with the right, the step being repeated once before the line moves off again.

(*b*) *jatra lujhri* (= *Jhumair*).—In the version which I saw in Jashpur *thana* the boys and girls hold hands and start the dance by walking briskly round the circle. There is then a brief reverse, the dancers walking backwards completing each pace with a hop (left foot one pace left foot hop; right foot one pace right foot hop). After this the line leaps into the main action. In the first figure the four movements consist of two brisk steps forward, the first with the right leg and the second with the left; the right foot then joins the left and both then jump together. In the second figure these movements are reversed—a pace back with the right leg being followed by a pace back with the left leg, then the right leg moves up to the left and finally there is a jump. The dance with its brisk march forward and the smart concluding jump has an angular vertical rhythm very different from the suave backwards and forwards swing of dances like the *Karam lujhki*. It is danced with a boisterous gusto.

(3) "TRANSITIONAL" SOCIAL DANCES

(*a*) *matha*.—This is a dance which is danced only by women and girls. In the Mandar version the dancers form a line round the circle facing the centre. The dance then starts with a pace forward with the left foot followed by first a jerking toss to the front with the right and then a jerking toss to the rear also with the right. The right leg is then brought down a little to the right and the left leg brought back to it. The left foot then moves forward and the kick-out and the kick-back with the right are repeated. In this way the line moves on in a series of tossing curves.

(*b*) *jadura.*—A *jadura* dance in the *thoriadeg* form at Mandar consists of little runs out with a leisured recoil and a drift round the circle. The boys and girls form two distinct lines facing inwards, the boys in front of the girls. Eight paces are smartly taken back. The steps then consist of three quick paces forward starting with the right, and then a lingering pace forward with the left. The right is then swung up to it, and the left leg then takes a long lunging pace back followed by a short step back by the right and a final short step back by the left. After this the run forward recurs, and so the dance goes on.

(*c*) *domkach.*—In the Jashpur version of the *domkach* the girls form a curved line facing the centre. The opening figure begins with a swinging run, the left leg taking a pace forward followed by the right. The left leg is then tossed forward and back. In the second figure the right foot comes back with a delayed swing, the left leg is brought across it, the right foot takes a further pace back and the figure closes with the left foot joining it. The swinging run then starts again, and in this way the line covers the circle. The *domkach* is a more deliberate and placid dance than either of the *lujhkis*—with a smooth "wave" action—a movement up to a graceful swaying toss, a recoil from it and again a movement up to the swaying toss.

(*d*) *dhuriya.*—In the Mandar versions of this dance the lines radiate from the centre like the spokes of a wheel. The boys and girls form distinct blocks, each block containing three or four lines, and each line eight to ten dancers. Six or eight "spokes" are therefore turning at a time. While the boys are dancing with a loose leaping swing, the girls move round behind deliberately and slowly. The steps of the girls consist of a pace forward with the right, followed by a pace forward with the left; the right is then brought up so that the feet are together and the line then leans forward.

In another version at Mandar three equal paces forward are taken commencing with the right foot, while the fourth step consists of a lingering slur forward by the left.

In the Jashpur versions the lines radiate from the centre. The dance begins by the lines marching forward. When the *or* is finished the dancers do a somewhat complicated movement consisting of a swing back followed by a sway back and then a sway forward. To execute it three paces back are taken in a run—the left foot taking the first, the right foot the second, and a hop by the right foot being added before the movement comes to rest with a third pace by the left foot. The right foot is then drawn back and advanced, the left is brought up to it and the right swung slightly forward. The line then marches on.

As a variation to the march the left foot is sometimes brought up to the right foot instead of going beyond it; and in another form a pause takes the place of the fourth step by the left foot.

(*d*) (1) *dhuriya lujhki.*—In the two Jashpur versions the dancers form a curving line facing the centre of the circle. In the first version the steps begin with a long pace sideways with the right foot. The left is then brought in front of it, and this is followed by a second long step sideways by the right. The left is then brought up to it. This is then partially reversed—the left foot taking a pace sideways to the left, the right being brought up in front of it, and the left being brought back with a hop. In this way the dance goes with a series of swinging hops.

In the second form the dancers face right, holding hands one behind the other. The first figure consists of three paces forward beginning with the right and is completed with a hop. The second consists of a hop with the left foot followed by paces forward with the right and left feet and ending in a hop on the right.

(*e*) *angani.*—In the Jashpur version the boys and girls form a mixed line facing the centre. The figure begins with a long pace back to the right with the right foot, the left foot is then brought across it with a swinging toss, the right foot then takes a swoop back and the left foot is drawn up to it. The left foot then takes a longish pace forward, the right foot is brought up behind it, the left is swung out and brought behind the right foot and the right foot then moves with a slight swing forward into a swoop to the right and back. The dance goes with a bending swing from the knees, accelerating into swinging hops as it works up.

(4) MARRIAGE DANCES

(*a*) *the "blessing" dance.*—This is described by Roy at page 298 of *The Oraons*. I have not myself seen this dance.

(*b*) *the marriage domkach.*—This is the "greeting" dance referred to in the account of the marriage procedure in Gumla *thana*. In a version which is danced in Jashpur during the course of the ceremony the boys and girls form a curved line facing the centre and the figure takes the following simple forms. The left leg is swung slightly back or simply lifted and then moves to the right in line with its original position. The right leg is then swung out and back. The dance moves deliberately, the emphasis falling on the careful swing of the right leg.

# INDEX